# THE SPIRIT OF THE GHETTO

*Bintel Briefs*

*Promised City*

by **HUTCHINS HAPGOOD**

*with drawings from life by*
**Jacob Epstein**

*New edition—preface and notes by*
**Harry Golden**

*Schocken Books* • *New York*

# THE SPIRIT OF THE GHETTO

Studies of the Jewish Quarter of New York

*A number of these chapters have appeared as separate
articles in* The Atlantic Monthly, The Critic, The Bookman,
The World's Work, The Boston Transcript, *and* The
Evening Post *and* The Commercial Advertiser *of New York.
To the editors of these publications, thanks for permission
to republish are gratefully tendered by the Author.*

*"The Nudnik" from* MORRIS ROSENFELD:
Selected Poetry and Prose, *Yiddisher
Kultur Farband, 1964, translated by
Max Rosenfeld. Reprinted by permission.*

*Designed by Adrianne Onderdonk*

# PREFACE

Hutchins Hapgood gathered the material for this book in the year 1901. Considering that the great mass of Jewish immigration from Eastern Europe had yet to come, that the ghetto was not yet a part of American life and history, Mr. Hapgood's insights stand up remarkably well. And the first published work of the artist-sculptor Jacob Epstein makes this a historic book. I am proud to have my name now joined with such men as Hapgood and Epstein in this new edition of their work, sixty-three years after its initial publication.

I have received close to a half-million letters during the past ten years as a result of my own recollections about New York's Jewish ghetto.* My correspondence has convinced me that there is much more involved in these recollections than nostalgia and sentimentality. It is interesting that Mr. Hapgood, a Gentile observer, got the point of this even before the New York ghetto reached its full development.

For sentimentality does not per se change the quality of life; indeed the chief objection to sentimentality is that it is a lie about the quality of life. The life portrayed here, and particularly the life implicit in Epstein's drawings, had a more hopeful quality, a richer texture, than

* The word "ghetto" is used throughout to denote a section of the city that is occupied, mostly out of economic necessity, by an immigrant or minority group—in this case, Jewish—not in the sense of a restricted prisonlike community.

the life the young folks see now stretching before them. On the Lower East Side in the early years of this century we came as close to any guarantee as life has ever offered. The guarantee was if you worked hard, went to school, studied and saved, you could participate in America.

Life offers no such guarantee today. There are millions of young people today unprepared and unfit to enter the automated industrial society of the 1960's. I need not repeat the cruel statistics of the number of college graduates who are doing jobs today that a generation ago were reserved for unlettered apprentices. Countless numbers of college graduates will retire from these jobs when they are sixty-five, where the unlettered apprentices moved onward and up.

We were poor on the Lower East Side of New York, very poor, far poorer I suspect than the poor in America now. But we had a strategy for defeating poverty. And many of us did defeat it. Those who did not may not have felt that life was fine and exquisite and brilliant— they may have felt life was hard and cruel but they did not feel it was empty, either. Life today contains a major problem in the ever-increasing segregation of the poor and the elderly. In the ghetto of New York, grandmothers and grandfathers and crotchety maiden aunts were a part of life, included in the whole. The old were ever-present. This is by and large not true today. The elderly live lonely lives in one housing development, and the young lead frenzied lives in another. We have telephones and radio and television, but communication between the age groups grows less and less distinct.

To be truthful, these things are felt and understood only in retrospect, and in retrospect I would say that I am happy to have grown up on the Lower East Side of New York. I believe it was a happier time to have grown to manhood than that in which my three sons grew to manhood. It was more vigorous, it contained a higher sense of involvement, and a wider feeling of hope.

A few statistics are necessary.

This book was published in 1902, and Mr. Hapgood spent the preceding year gathering his material. But the bulk of the immigration of Eastern European Jews to the Lower East Side of New York came in 1904, 1905, 1906, 1907, and 1908, when a total of seven hundred thousand Jewish immigrants poured through Ellis Island. It is important to remember Mr. Hapgood is not talking about the flux at its crest but at its beginnings.

Next to the Italians, the Jews constituted the second largest group of immigrants between 1899 and 1914. And Jewish immigration did not, as did others, diminish in times of depression in America.

The largest year of Jewish immigration was 1906, the year of the worst Cossack raids on Jewish villages in Russia. The total Jewish immigration, from 1899 to the beginning of World War I in 1914, was 1,532,690. Almost all these Jewish immigrants settled permanently in the United States. Among Jewish immigrants there was always a large number of women and children, forty-four Jewish women to every fifty-six Jewish men, and twenty-four children under fourteen to every seventy-six adults. More than a million Jewish women and children (654,080 and 362,073 respectively) followed husbands and fathers and brothers to the New World, more women and children than any other immigrant group. These statistics can readily be confirmed in the *Universal Jewish Encyclopedia,* and at the Jewish Information Bureau of New York, and also in the annual yearbook of the American Jewish Committee.

Most of the immigrants were poor. A slim 7 percent had fifty dollars on their arrival and 38 percent had less than fifty dollars. And 55 percent had no money at all. The average money a Jewish immigrant might have was fifteen dollars and fifty cents compared to a general average of twenty-two dollars among other immigrants. This low figure was due, however, to the great number of Jewish women and children. Nearly 70 percent of all the Jewish immigrants to America in those years paid for their journey with money borrowed from relatives. (Thousands of the non-Jewish immigrants were imported by native Americans to fill a growing labor market.)

The First World War put a halt to Jewish immigration from 1914 to 1920. From July 1, 1914, to June 30, 1919, the total number of Jewish immigrants was only 65,764, which included some 20,000 from Canada. After the war, Jewish immigration swelled to new proportions. In 1921 more than 120,000 came to America. This figure dropped to less than half in 1922 with the introduction of the first immigrant quota system to be passed into law by Congress.

While the Lower East Side was a voluntary ghetto, it was composed of six or seven smaller ghettos contained within the larger one. Geographically, the whole ghetto of New York was the square mile below Fourteenth Street between the East and Hudson rivers. These blocks bordering the East River were populated by Italians, and along the blocks bordering the Hudson River lived the Irish. I have always wondered why so few Jewish boys learned to swim. With the Italians and the Irish holding the river beachheads, the Jews were landlocked. So they devoted their energies to basketball and boxing, which they could practice in the settlement houses, in the basements, and on the tenement roofs.

Soon the Italians began to spill into the Jewish section. Even in my day Italians were already living on Chrystie Street, the first street eastward from the Bowery. As the Italians moved in, the Jews moved out. After the Williamsburg Bridge was completed at Delancey and Clinton streets, Jews by the thousands moved across the river into the Williamsburg section of Brooklyn.

Throughout the Lower East Side there were whole

tenements of Poles who we were led to believe were nat-
ural-born anti-Semites. Most of the stories I heard as a
boy about anti-Semitism in Europe involved the Polish
peasants. It is interesting that when the Poles came to
America, with the entire continent open to them, so
many thousands of them settled among the Jews again.

Though surrounded by Poles and Italians, it was the
Irish and the Irish alone we Jews admired. It wasn't that
the Irish were earlier immigrants. Indeed not. It was that
we identified the Irishman not only with the English
language but also with the image of what an American
should look like. The Irish were the cops and the firemen
and the ballplayers. Although the immigrant Jew and the
Irish poor did not get along well, these Irish were still
figures Jewish immigrants wanted to emulate. I saw
Orthodox Jewish women literally jump for joy at the
birth of a grandson, and say, "He looks just like an Irishman."

It was the Irish who instructed us in one part of the
legacy of the ghetto. The legacy was that we could proceed outward as they had. For by the time we occupied
the tenements that soared to meet us, many of the Irish
had moved inland to The Bronx, to New Jersey, to Chicago, and points west. The other part of the legacy we
brought from the old country. This was our Jewishness,
the fact positive that we were immigrants. In one sense
or another, Jews are always "immigrants"; "eternal al-
iens" perhaps, which confers upon them a special and
intellectual vigor, the key to Jewish survival through
twenty centuries. Immigrants came off the gangplank at
Ellis Island, looked into the faces of passing Americans,
and said, "When will I look like one of them?" The reason for the Jew's everlasting vitality is that even after a
third generation he's still striving to "be like one of
them," and dares not relax his strivings for a single moment.

My family lived in the heart of the Lower East Side,

the Times Square of the ghetto—171 Eldridge Street, between Rivington and Delancey streets. In those days, one tenement faced away from another, separated in the rear by a backyard about twenty feet wide. The toilets for both tenements were located in this yard, five of them usually strung together, each about the size of a telephone booth. If you lifted the board in one, the board in all came up, which led to constant arguments always echoing from one booth to the other. Once a month, Poles in hip boots came and cleaned these privies. Later on came the inside toilets, one to a floor, serving four families. And I want you to understand that I am talking about substantial families—father, mother, approximately five children, and three boarders.

The rent in the back apartments was considerably less than the twenty-two dollars we paid for four rooms in the front on the top floor.

It was with a tenant in the back that I made my first contact with death. A man in one of the rear tenements died when the fumes from his coal stove overcame him one night. He was a ragpicker. I had seen him every day carrying huge sacks on his back, and I could see him at night, sitting in his flat in the back sorting the rags he had collected into a dozen different piles, according to size, quality, and color. Each of these piles was bundled and sold.

The police came and carried him down the stairs on a stretcher. On the ground floor they were met by a weary looking woman in tears—the ragpicker's daughter who kept wailing as the grim cops marched to the street. Later three bearded Jews came and cleaned out his room. They were members of the fraternal society to which he belonged, which provided burial insurance, plus a twenty-dollar "benefit" toward the cost of the gravestone. No Jew, not even the poorest of the poor, was ever buried by the city in Potter's Field. All the Jews would have lost face.

"The New York ghetto," wrote Hapgood in 1902, "is constantly changing. It shifts from one part of town to another, and the time is not so far distant when it will cease to exist altogether."

Not too long ago I stood in the doorway of a tenement on the Lower East Side of New York and looked at the flights of stairs my mother had climbed so often with her black leather market bag.

I felt sad for a moment. I'd been back before a few times, but I hadn't really explored the neighborhood for nearly forty years. There have been many changes, of course. The elevated structures of the Bowery and First Avenue are gone and there are a few new housing developments. But what is amazing is that so much of it is exactly as I knew it as a boy down there before World War I. Our old home at 171 Eldridge Street—a cold-water tenement house that must have been thirty years old in 1905—is still full of tenants.

I examined the names in the mailboxes of the tenement of today, and where once there had been Rabinowitz and Cohen there were now Perez and Amici. And as I stood in that hallway which had been my own for my first fifteen years, the Negro and Puerto Rican kids looked at me as if I had just dropped down from the planet Mars.

You can write a social history of our country by walking through a neighborhood. First were the Germans, then the Irish, the Jews, the Italians, and now the Negroes and the Puerto Ricans, and each group leaves its deposits for the future and stores away its memories. What manner of children, of what nationality and history, will be staring at the "stranger" when the Puerto Rican actor or Negro vice president of the United States comes back fifty years from now?

Hutchins Hapgood and his contemporaries, Jacob A. Riis and Lincoln Steffens, and later on Carl Sandburg, were the first "outside" observers to recognize that the Jewish immigrant had brought a special quality with him. Hapgood called it "the spirit of the ghetto." It was an intellectual vitality we do not feel today, precisely the special quality which has since made the Jew in America the subject of a vast literature.

There was a great desire to learn. It began when the young boy was wrapped in the prayer cloth for his first Hebrew lesson. The mother dropped a coin on the page as he concentrated, then told him an angel left it as his reward for passing his first lesson.

The ghetto calls back to me the memory of quiet holidays, and on every second block the sign LECTURE TONIGHT, and the technical schools, the kind the educational experts of today want for all America.

Two weeks before the High Holy Days, there were no factory workers, or scholars, or peddlers or teachers; there were only Jews preparing for the annual period of rededication. On the first night of the High Holy Days, the streets were silent, dark, deserted. All year there had been the clamor of voices arguing over purchases, shouting from windows, a million sounds in different dialects and accents. Now the street stands were boarded up, the stores were shuttered. Everyone was home around the table. The Lower East Side spent the day in prayer.

There were fellows on the East Side selling candy and seltzer ("for two cents plain" or with syrup for three cents) who had lending libraries. The standard book was *David Copperfield;* another was *Les Misérables.* Several Russian and German novels translated into Yiddish were also staples. A fifteen-cent deposit and a nickel for two weeks was the charge. The seltzer fellow thumbed through books to see all the pages were still intact, none defaced, before he returned the deposit.

But could this have been truly a happy time? Have some of us overromanticized the ghetto of New York's

Lower East Side? The garbage littered the streets. The tenements could not be heated in the winter and were brutal in the summer. The poverty was all-encompassing. Peddlers with a houseful of children checked in their pushcarts at ten o'clock at night, went home and put the day's earnings on the table—all two dollars and seventy cents of it in coins—and the peddler and his wife laughed and told jokes to celebrate this good fortune. My mother walked from Eldridge and Rivington streets to the market under the Williamsburg Bridge, a distance of one mile each way; she made that trip twice a week because butter was one penny cheaper there—one penny cheaper. But our life was measured in those pennies. And in a section with a vast network of settlement houses and self-help societies, there was also a Jewish Desertion Bureau, where abandoned wives with their children sat all day on hard wooden benches waiting for a scrap of information.

Then what makes so many of the people in this affluent land write me about the ghetto with such genuine affection? Eric Hoffer, the writer, may have put his finger on it when he said, "The ghetto was a fortress as much as it was a prison." Our ghetto was indeed a fortress. And a prison, too. But a prison out of which a man could escape any time he had the will to. *This was the great challenge—to get out*. And life is a series of challenges, the greater they are, the better for all of us.

And the Jews prepared for the challenge, as always, with humor. The East Side literally rocked with humor. Looking back upon it it is still to me the wonder of wonders—the puns, the laughter, the thousands of jokes. Not strange at all that for the next two generations all America was entertained by Jewish comedians—*comikers* as we called them. The ghetto poor laughed fit to be tied at the rich German Jews uptown, but they joked about everything: about the tough Irish cops, about the dirt-filled alleys and the sweatshops, even about the terrible ghetto disease that afflicted so many of them—tuberculosis. They called it "Jewish asthma."

But mostly they joked about their own ambivalence, the contradictory forces that governed their lives: the self-hatred and the conceit, the deep nostalgia for the Orthodox ways of their parents, and the terrific drive to be like the tall, blue-eyed, blond Irishman.

The ghetto humor was usually in form of a *vitz*, a philosophical witticism (its diminutive, a *vitzl*, was a little joke, a pun). Often intellectuals in the coffee house carried on entire conversations in puns, jokes, and just plain fun.

An old *vitz* recites the story of the lion that escaped from the traveling circus and sent the panic-stricken ghetto running for safety. An elderly Jew comes out of his cobbler's shop and asks what's the matter. He is told a lion is in the streets, so he asks quite naturally, "Is it good for the Jews or bad for the Jews?"

The Jewish Captain Dreyfus is convicted in a Paris court and a mob smashes the windows of Jewish merchants in Algiers. The Jew even saw the humor implicit in anti-Semitism—the complete renunciation of logic that is necessary for a man to maintain himself as an anti-Semite and retain a degree of sanity at the same time.

Interestingly enough the ghetto Jew never asked for sympathy, and, above everything else, he was rarely a bore.

I recall the peddler who read books all day standing beside his pushcart, and how rude he was to a customer. The nerve of her! What an intrusion! And there was a fellow with a stall selling scholarly books in the Hebrew language. He gave every would-be customer an oral examination before he'd let him buy a book. The customer picked up a volume and the proprietor immediately put two or three scholarly questions to him. If he was dissatisfied with the answers he would shake his head, but he'd be gentle about it, "Leave the book here, it's not for you, it's not for you."

And where else but in the Jewish ghetto could the beggar be elevated to a self-contained aristocracy? The *schnorrer* is indeed a beggar who lives on handouts, traveling from one synagogue to another, from one businessman to another. He is always adamant, indignant, and overbearing. He is sure his patrons need him more than he needs his patrons. "If not for me," says the *schnorrer*, "how else could you, the giver of alms, accumulate the necessary quota of *mitzvahs*, the good deeds to be added up on the day of final reckoning?"

There were hundreds of *schnorrers* in the ghetto. A few are still around. Only a few years ago I met one who came to my office in Charlotte. It was late fall and so he was on his way to Florida. I registered him in a downtown hotel. I told the clerk I wanted a single room and (the ghetto humor still lives) the *schnorrer* interrupted, "with a shower and television, please." The rabbi took care of the *schnorrer* for breakfast, the owner of the big ready-to-wear shop supplied the lunch, and the treasurer of the temple saw him to the bus station.

But let us get on with Mr. Hapgood's observations of sixty-three years ago. I understand that Mr. Hapgood was still living in the Lower East Side's University Settlement House when I started to go there at the age of seven in 1910. And now we "meet" in this book, but we may have passed each other fifty-five years ago—in the corridors or maybe on the big staircase.

*Harry Golden*
*1965*

# FOREWORD

The Jewish quarter of New York is generally supposed to be a place of poverty, dirt, ignorance and immorality—the seat of the sweatshop, the tenement house, where "red lights" sparkle at night, where the people are queer and repulsive. Well-to-do persons visit the ghetto merely from motives of curiosity or philanthropy; writers treat of it sociologically, as of a place in crying need of improvement.

That the ghetto has an unpleasant aspect is as true as it is trite. But the unpleasant aspect is not the subject of the following sketches. I was led to spend much time in certain poor resorts of Yiddish New York not through motives either philanthropic or sociological, but simply by virtue of the charm I felt in men and things there. East Canal Street and the Bowery have interested me more than Broadway and Fifth Avenue. Why, the reader may learn from the present volume—which is an attempt made by a Gentile to report sympathetically on the character, lives and pursuits of certain East Side Jews with whom he has been in relations of considerable intimacy.

*Hutchins Hapgood*
*1902*

# CONTENTS

# THE SPIRIT OF THE GHETTO

*The old man*

# one

# THE OLD AND THE NEW

### THE OLD MAN

No part of New York has a more intense and varied life than the colony of Russian and Galician Jews who live on the East Side and who form the largest Jewish city in the world. The old and the new come here into close contact and throw each other into high relief. The traditions and customs of the Ortho-dox Jew are maintained almost in their purity, and opposed to these are forms and ideas of modern life of the most extreme kind. The Jews are at once tenacious of their character and susceptible to their Gentile environment, when that environment is of a high order of civilization. Accordingly, in enlightened America they undergo rapid transformation though retaining much that is distinctive, while in Russia, surrounded by an ignorant peasantry, they remain by themselves, do not so commonly learn the Gentile language, and prefer their own forms of culture. There their life centers about religion. Prayer and the study of the Law constitute practically the whole life of the religious Jew.

When the Jew comes to America he remains, if he is old, essentially the same as he was in Russia.

It is a tribute to Mr. Hapgood's understanding that he saw this development so clearly. The Jewish immigrants from Russia, Poland, Austria, Hungary, Rumania, and Lithuania, who were the vanguard of this exodus, came here because they were persecuted in the old country— persecuted first by laws that made them third-class citizens, and second, by the threat of physical violence that kept them and their women and children in constant peril.

The immigrant Jews were poor, true. But they did not emigrate to America because of poverty as did most of the other nineteenth-century immigrants, many of whom always thought of someday returning to the homeland. And before World War I, many of these immigrants did return; America was simply an economic adventure to them. But surprisingly few Jews went back, less than 4 percent, as compared to 19 percent for the Italians. And half of the Jewish 4 percent emigrated to Palestine, which was not a return to the old country at all.

In fact, one of the arguments presented by the proponents of the restrictive immigration bills to President Woodrow Wilson was that immigrants did go home, taking millions of American dollars with them. These Congressmen showed President Wilson the statistics that had been compiled on Italian returnees. Wilson vetoed the bill, remarking, "They left us the subways and tunnels they built, didn't they?"

But the Jews came to America to establish a new life. My mother told me that her life in Europe, though no idyl, was infinitely preferable to life in the New York ghetto. She told me of the joys of walking barefoot through the meadows of her village in Rumania. She told me of the beauties of the wheat fields and the distant mountains. In our ghetto tenement the halls stank, and through our front window we looked out upon a string of horse stables. Despite this, my mother said, she was happy that there was a new life for her children. Here in America they had opportunity.

Life was pleasant, healthier, and more beautiful in the old country perhaps, but it always contained the seeds of menace and deprivation. No Jewish boy, she told me, no matter how smart, could expect to rise higher than apothecary, and that only by sufferance, special permission, and bribery. The crowded tenement was worth it, she said. My mother was smart though she could neither read nor write. In the synagogue, which she attended regularly, she repeated the prayers by rote and from memory.

---

His deeply rooted habits and the "worry of daily bread" make him but little sensitive to the conditions of his new home. His imagination lives in the old country and he gets his consolation in the old religion. He picks up only about a hundred English words and phrases, which he pronounces in his own way. Some of his most common acquisitions are *vinda* (window), *zieling* (ceiling), *never mind, alle right, that'll do, politzman* (policeman), *ein schön kind, ein reg'lar pitze!* (a pretty child, a regular picture). Of this modest vocabulary he is very proud, for it takes him out of the category of the "greenhorn"— a term of contempt to which the satirical Jew is very sensitive.

---

The system in most households was fixed and simple. The parents spoke Yiddish to the children who answered in English. This system gave rise to the ghetto proverb "In America the children bring up the parents."

Most parents doubted they could manage English. They had no idea they were even remotely familiar with the language. But their Yiddish sentences were filled with such words as *haircut, school, grocery, boarder, wedding, factory, teacher, office, doctor, automobile, medicine, telephone, drugstore,* and other nouns that described the appurtenances of daily living.

The Yiddish accent and the grotesque pronunciation became a source of humor, a standard feature in vaudeville in the person of the stage Jew. But before long the dialect joke had become an anachronism. The dialect jokes began to make little sense when the "greenhorn's" grandson was in medical school and his granddaughter was up at Radcliffe.

---

The man who has been only three weeks in this country hates few things so much as to be called a greenhorn. Under this fear he learns the small vocabulary to which in many years he adds very little. His dress receives rather greater modification than his language. In the old country he never appeared in a short coat; that would be enough to stamp him as a free thinker. But when he comes to New York and his coat is worn out, he is unable to find any garment long enough. The best he can do is to buy a cutaway, or a Prince Albert, which he often calls a Prince Isaac. As soon as he imbibes the fear of being called a greenhorn he assumes the Prince Isaac with less regret. Many of the old women, without diminution of piety, discard their wigs, which are strictly required by the Orthodox in Russia, and go even to the synagogue with nothing on their heads but their natural locks.

---

Assimilation was the overriding influence on the entire Jewish immigrant culture. Everyone dreaded the epithet greenhorn, and immigrants who had arrived in April were not above calling the July arrivals greenhorns and mocking them. The drive to become an American demanded a schoolboy speak English to his parents. And the schoolboy often insisted, as I insisted, that his father either trim his beard in the manner of President Ulysses S. Grant or General Robert E. Lee or shave the beard off once and for all.

Clothing played a big role in this desire for assimilation. Any clothes that looked American were desired, and nothing set off this American style like a gold watch and chain. The watch and chain were the ne plus ultra in Americanization. Peddlers who extended credit did a flourishing business with new immigrants, selling the men the watch and chain and selling the women the delicate gold watch with a fleur-de-lis pin to hold it on the bosom.

One of our relatives arrived from Ellis Island carrying an alarm clock. He had bought it from a peddler for a dollar and ninety-five cents less than an hour after the immigration officials had passed him through.

The immigrants on the East Side did indeed have a foot in two worlds. An early friend of the newcomer was the Tammany Hall worker who advised him about first papers for citizenship, and night study classes, and then the immigrant, if he was a *singlemon* (unmarried), met the *shadkhan* (the marriage broker).

The East Side Jews were especially alert about the opportunities of their new environment. When someone asked the immigrant mother, "How old are your children?" she would reply with confidence and dignity, "The doctor is four and the lawyer is two and a half."

---

The old Jew on arriving in New York usually becomes a sweatshop tailor or pushcart peddler. There are few more pathetic sights than an old man with a long beard, a little black cap on his head and a vener-

*Old scholar turned beggar*

able face—a man who had been perhaps a Hebraic or Talmudic scholar in the old country—carrying or pressing piles of coats in the melancholy sweatshop, or standing for sixteen hours a day by his pushcart in one of the dozen crowded streets of the ghetto, where the great markets are, selling among many other things apples, garden stuff, fish, and second-hand shirts.

There were also door-to-door peddlers on the Lower East Side. The fellow put his pack on the floor in front of him and knocked on the door of the tenement flat.

The woman answered and he said, "Missus, you light the Sabbath candles this Friday at twelve minutes after six, and I wish you a good Sabbath. Perhaps you need a few candles? No? A bread knife?" He went through his entire inventory. Finally when the woman said she needed nothing, he strapped the pack on his back, extended his palm and asked, "Maybe you can give a Jew something for the Sabbath?"

Occupations, as Hapgood describes them, reflected the social structure of the Jewish population in Eastern Europe. In Hapgood's time, there was still within the immigrant community a relatively high proportion of Jews without occupations. There were two reasons for this: a large number of the Jews were women and children, and the Jewish social structure of Eastern Europe that freed the "scholar" from the need of an occupation. I remember the teacher asking an immigrant boy, "What does your father do?" and the boy answered with a look of surprise, *"Eir learent"* (he's reading the books of the prophets). What a question!

It was a great shock, a disintegrating blow, to these men to learn that the American social structure was based on earnings, on money. Many of these men were past middle age. Not only could they not learn an occupation, but their prestige diminished year by year. My father, who was one of these "readers," once complained with contempt, "In America the *balagoola* [really means ignoramous] becomes the president of the *shul*." I recall a humiliating experience in connection with one of these scholars who lost status in America. During a heated discussion at a fraternal-society meeting, a peddler, who had become a wholesaler, waved his finger in my father's face and shouted; "Reb Lebche, in Europe when you saw me coming you walked on the other side of the street; in America when I see you coming, *I* walk on the other side of the street." For many of the immigrants it was the story of America in a nutshell and it came from a peddler-advanced-to-wholesaler. Jacob Epstein has sketched two of these lost souls in America (in the drawing he appropriately calls "Submerged Scholars").

The accelerated pace of the American drive for status through money swept up all the Jews soon enough. By World War I, even some of the "readers" were in trade —peddling, teaching, selling door-to-door; many of them became *shadkhans;* some functioned as rabbis without benefit of formal ordination. My father, the "reader," eventually wrote free-lance articles for the Yiddish press and also got a license to perform civil marriages; thus he was able to contribute to the family income an average of about five hundred dollars a year. He also made the charity-drive speeches at the theater benefits for his fraternal society.

Despite the "readers," the proportion of skilled workers among Jews was the largest among any immigrant group—50 percent. The Jews were needle-trade workers, cobblers, milliners, furriers and the like; many, many of them were, as Hapgood points out, tailors. According to the *Universal Jewish Encyclopedia,* the Jewish immigration at the beginning of the century created the ready-made clothing industry of the United States. In 1889, Americans spent four hundred and forty million dollars for ready-made clothing; in 1914, gross sales in this industry were up to one billion three hundred million dollars.

The drive of most was to become self-employed. As yet they were unemployable in the open society. They lacked the ability to speak the English language, and they wanted to observe the Sabbath and the many Holy Days during the year. For the vast number of Jews from Eastern Europe were Orthodox. Their livelihood had to permit them to go home before sundown on Friday to prepare to observe the Sabbath on Saturday and go to work, if possible, on Sunday. Obviously they could do this conveniently as entrepreneurs, self-employed. So they became manufacturers and peddlers, or contractors for manufacturers, or they worked for other Jews.

I remember many factories that closed down on Friday

afternoon and remained shut on Saturday and this was in the days of the ten-hour day, six-day week.

But the desire for self-employment went far beyond the need to observe the Sabbath. Involved also was the Jew's suspicion that he would perhaps remain unemployable for at least a full generation. A cousin of mine manufactured men's shirts in a small shop. He employed three female seamstresses. The fellow could barely speak a dozen words of English but he filled orders that came from Macy's. Had my cousin presented himself at Macy's—and I mean no disrespect for that great enterprise—he would never have been hired. Not only did he "look" entirely different from most of their employees, he could not understand the language. So instead of presenting *himself* at the employment office of R. H. Macy, my cousin sent a sample of his work to their buying office. Thus, he was actually "employed" by them for many years.

The self-employed often manufactured garments in the tenement flats in which they lived. During the day the front room, bedroom, and kitchen became a whirling, churning factory, where men, women, and children worked at the sewing and pressing machines.

In one room would be four men, one or two women, a couple of young girls, aged nine to fourteen, and perhaps an eleven-year-old boy, working on knickerbockers or knee pants.

It was all piecework. They averaged about seventy-five cents for a dozen pairs which would leave a family of five with about fifteen dollars a week. The hot irons were on the stove in the heat of the summer (the busy season for the knee pants workers), so that the presser, usually the father or one of the male boarders, would always have one available. The young girls and often the wife were all considered "learners," which enabled everybody to circumvent whatever laws were on the books.

The boarders paid two dollars and fifty cents a week

for sleeping accommodations and breakfast, and everybody worked twelve hours a day, the goal being to turn out fifteen to twenty dozen pairs of knee pants. The eleven-year-old would barely earn enough from a week's work to buy one pair of knee pants for himself.

And, of course, this work was seasonal. Five months of the year the machines were silent, the knee pants workers idle. Many of the men carried their own machines and went from factory to factory asking for a day's work. The average pay of the family often went as high as twenty-five dollars a week, if they worked from seven in the morning to eleven at night. A few blocks farther north, on Stanton Street, were the tenements where the experienced tailors were working, where whole families worked together to make men's coats that would earn for them an average of twenty-seven cents a coat. Each was delivered to the contractor with all operations complete except for buttons and buttonholes, which the contractor would let our elsewhere.

Many of these people wept when the industry, in 1912-1914, became unionized. They were afraid they would lose their livelihood. In such ways does poverty feed upon itself. Free enterprise existed in its purest state on the Lower East Side of New York and principally among the Jews, who knew all about living in a competitive world.

The unskilled, of course, took to peddling, peddling with a pushcart. They sold everything under the sun from those pushcarts. Tin cups cost two cents a piece, peaches a penny a quart, hats a quarter, and eyeglasses thirty-five cents a pair. The eyeglass peddler had a mirror attached to a stick for the fitting of a customer. A pair of eyeglasses was a big item among the immigrants. The hope of every immigrant boy was to be a scholar, a learned man, and eyeglasses were a start. The photographers kept boxes of eyeglasses as props for customers when they came to have their pictures taken.

The peddlers also sold chickens and geese hung from carts by the neck. A housewife bought a half or a quarter of a chicken, and many of those who could not afford a whole one bought smaller pieces for the Sabbath meal.

Up and down the street was a peddler churning horse radish on a machine that he usually padlocked to a lamp-post to prevent its theft.

And the streets always echoed to the calls of the sus-pender peddler, who carried his wares over his shoulder —and when it rained he sold umbrellas.

The early Hebrews acquired their knowledge of busi-ness and trade from the neighboring peoples, particularly the Phoenicians and Carthaginians. But, as Miriam Beard of Princeton pointed out in her book, *Jews in a Gentile World,* the Jews never had a business empire and that may be another secret of their survival. Dr. Beard says that business empires, like other empires, crumble and decay; rich businessmen grow soft and lose initiative and the power to defend themselves. No soci-ety has ever enjoyed a commercial supremacy twice. Dr. Beard adds that one might argue that the reason for the Jewish survival has been that they never had business supremacy in the countries in which they lived. Small business success, yes—like that on the Lower East Side; but supremacy, never—fortunately.

---

The old Jew also becomes a member of one of the many hundred lodges which exist on the East Side. These societies curiously express at once the old Jew-ish customs and the conditions of the new world. They are mutual-insurance companies formed to sup-port sick members. When a brother is ill, the presi-dent appoints a committee to visit him. Mutual-insurance societies and committees are American enough, and visiting the sick is prescribed by the Talmud. This is a striking instance of the adaptation of the old to the new. The committee not only condoles with the decrepit member but gives him a sum of money.

---

Since Mr. Hapgood's day, whole books have been devoted to the history of the *Landsmanschaften*—fraternal societies formed by Jews who emigrated from the same area or place in Europe.

The most important of these *Landsmanschaften* in New York City was chartered in 1864 as the Bialystoker Mutual Aid Society. Bialystok was the home of the famous breakfast roll as well as the birthplace of the actor Gregory Ratoff, of sacred memory. By 1877, there were twenty-two major Eastern European societies in New York City as well as dozens of smaller *vereins,* self-help societies providing small loans and paying funeral "benefits." My father belonged to the Mikulinczer *verein.* We had come from Mikulincze, a small Jewish village in Galicia in the Austro-Hungarian empire. (My mother was born in Mihalen, a Jewish village across the border in Rumania.)

Another of these great self-help organizations was the Hebrew Free Loan Society on Second Avenue. It was founded in 1892 on a capital investment of ninety-five dollars. It granted loans of up to five hundred dollars to people, whether employed or not, and made these loans without an investigation or a demand for collateral. It only required the endorsement of two responsible persons who had bank accounts or who did business in Greater New York.

The borrower had to promise to repay his loan within ten months. The Hebrew Free Loan Society has had a fantastic record of repayments. Its seventy-three year history has seen forty-five million dollars loaned to eight hundred thousand borrowers. Though the Jews on the Lower East Side lived amid grinding poverty, they were proud that they depended neither on city nor private charity, being able to make do on their own.

The Jews brought this idea of organized self-help to America out of the ghetto and Pale of Settlement in Europe. Some of the principles of these *vereins* are now familiar to all Americans: social security, community chest, unemployment benefits, sick leave, medical insurance. For almost all of these *vereins* were in essence mutual-insurance companies and most of them were established on solid foundations. Years later when New York State enacted a more stringent insurance code, most of these societies were approved for continued operation.

These societies and *vereins* provided a sophisticated program of "medicare" for the entire family. Young doctors often vied with one another for election as the *verein* doctor. In the *verein* to which our family subscribed, we paid fifty cents every two months, which provided us with medical care when we needed it as well as a flat cost of fifty cents for prescriptions. There was a special tax for confinement cases. Eight dollars. Imagine that. Eight dollars.

The solicitors for the society never sold memberships on the provision that ". . . in the event of your death, your family will need. . . ." They sold "benefits" and "benefits" only. The most famous English word in the ghetto was "benefits," which replaced such words as "death," "sickness," and "unemployment." It was a way to deceive the Evil Eye! "If, God forbid, something should happen, the 'benefit' will give your wife. . . ."

---

Another way in which the life of the old Jew is affected by his New York environment, perhaps the most important was as far as intellectual and educative influences are concerned, is through the Yiddish newspapers, which exist nowhere except in this country. They keep him in touch with the world's happenings in a way quite impossible in Europe. At the Yiddish theaters, too, he sees American customs portrayed, although grotesquely, and the old Orthodox things often satirized to a degree, the greenhorn laughed to scorn, and the rabbi held up to derision.

Nevertheless, these influences leave the man pretty much as he was when he landed here. He remains the patriarchal Jew devoted to the Law and to prayer. He never does anything that is not prescribed, and worships most of the time that he is not at work. He has only one point of view, that of the Talmud; and his esthetic as well as his religious criteria are determined by it. "This is a beautiful letter you have written me," wrote an old man to his son. "It smells of Isaiah." He makes of his house a synagogue, and prays three times a day; when he prays, his head is covered, he wears the black and white praying shawl, and the cubes of the phylactery are attached to his forehead and left arm. To the cubes are fastened two straps of goatskin, black and white; those on the forehead hang down, and those attached to the other cube are wound seven times about the left arm. Inside each cube is a white parchment on which is written the Hebrew word for God, which must never be spoken by a Jew. The strength of this prohibition is so great that even the Jew who has lost his faith is unwilling to pronounce the word.

Besides the home prayers there are daily visits to the synagogue, fasts and holidays to observe. When there is a death in the family the Jew does not go to

Day of Atonement

the synagogue, but prays at home. The ten men necessary for the funeral ceremony, who are partly supplied by the bereavement committee of the lodge, sit seven days in their stocking feet on footstools and read Job all the time. On the Day of Atonement the old Jew stands much of the day in the synagogue, wrapped in a white gown, and seems to be one of a meeting of the dead. The Day of Rejoicing of the Law and the Day of Purim are the only two days in the year when an Orthodox Jew may be intoxicated. It is virtuous on these days to drink too much, but the sobriety of the Jew is so great that he sometimes cheats his friends and himself by shamming drunkenness. On the first and second evenings of the Passover the father dresses in a big white robe, the family gathers about him, and the youngest male child asks the father the reason why the day is celebrated. Whereupon the old man relates the whole history, and they all talk it over and eat, and drink wine, but in no vessel which has been used before during the year, for everything must be fresh and clean on this day. The night before the Passover the remaining leavened bread is gathered together, just enough for breakfast, for only unleavened bread can be eaten during the next eight days. The head of the family goes around with a candle, gathers up the crumbs with a quill or a spoon, and burns them. A custom which has almost died out in New York is for the congregation to go out of the synagogue on the night of the full moon, and chant a prayer in the moonlight.

In addition to daily religious observances in his home and in the synagogues, to fasts and holidays, the Orthodox Jew must give much thought to his diet. One great law is the line drawn between milk things and meat things. The Bible forbids boiling a kid in the milk of its mother. Consequently the hairsplitting Talmud prescribes the most farfetched discrimination. For instance, a plate in which meat is cooked is called a meat vessel, the knife with which it is cut is called a meat knife, the spoon with which one eats the soup that was cooked in a meat pot, though there is no meat in the soup, is a meat spoon, and to use that spoon for a milk thing is prohibited. All these regulations, of course, seem privileges to the Orthodox Jew. The sweatshops are full of religious fanatics, who, in addition to their ceremonies at home, form Talmudic clubs and gather in tenement-house rooms, which they convert into synagogues.

In several of the cafés of the quarter these old fellows gather. With their long beards, long black coats, and serious demeanor, they sit about little tables and drink honey cider, eat lima beans, and jealously exclude from their society the socialists and freethink-

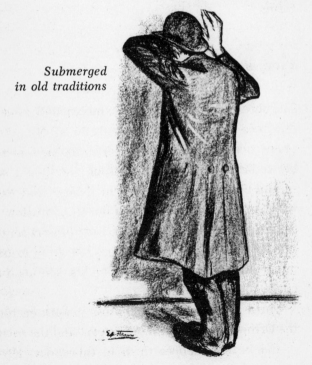

*Submerged
in old traditions*

ers of the colony who, not unwillingly, have cafés of their own. They all look poor, and many of them are, in fact, peddlers, shopkeepers, or tailors; but some, not distinguishable in appearance from the proletarians, have "made their pile." Some are Hebrew scholars, some of the older class of Yiddish journalists. There are no young people there, for the young bring irreverence and the American spirit, and these cafés are strictly Orthodox.

In spite, therefore, of his American environment, the old Jew of the ghetto remains patriarchal, highly trained and educated in a narrow sectarian direction, but entirely ignorant of modern culture—medieval, in effect, submerged in old tradition and outworn forms.

### THE BOY

The shrewd-faced boy with the melancholy eyes that one sees everywhere in the streets of New York's ghetto occupies a peculiar position in our society. If we could penetrate into his soul, we should see a mixture of almost unprecedented hope and excitement on the one hand, and of doubt, confusion, and self-distrust on the other hand. Led in many contrary directions, the fact that he does not grow to be an intellectual anarchist is due to his serious racial characteristics.

Three groups of influences are at work on him—the Orthodox Jewish, the American. and the socialist—and he experiences them in this order. He has

*Morning prayer*

either been born in America of Russian-Austrian-, or Rumanian-Jewish parents, or has emigrated with them when a very young child. The first of the three forces at work on his character is religious and moral; the second is practical, diversified, nonreligious; the third is reactionary from the other two and hostile to them.

Whether born in this country or in Russia, the son of Orthodox parents passes his earliest years in a family atmosphere, where the whole duty of man is to observe the religious Law. He learns to say his prayers every morning and evening, either at home or at the synagogue. At the age of five, he is taken to the

*The* chaider

Hebrew private school, the *chaider*, where, in Russia, he spends most of his time from early morning till late at night. The ceremony accompanying his first appearance in *chaider* is significant of his whole Orthodox life. Wrapped in a *talith* (praying shawl), he is carried by his father to the school and received there by the *melamed* (teacher), who holds out before him the Hebrew alphabet on a large chart. Before beginning to learn the first letter of the alphabet, he is given a taste of honey, and when he declares it to be sweet, he is told that the study of the holy Law, upon which he is about to enter, is sweeter than honey. Shortly afterward a coin falls from the ceiling, and the boy is told that an angel dropped it from heaven as a reward for learning the first lesson.

In the Russian *chaider* the boy proceeds with a further study of the alphabet, then of the prayer book, the Pentateuch, other portions of the Bible, and finally begins with the complicated Talmud. Confirmed at thirteen years of age, he enters the Hebrew academy and continues the study of the Talmud, to which, if he is successful, he will devote himself all his life. For his parents desire him to be a rabbi, or a Talmudical scholar, and to give himself entirely to a learned interpretation of the sweet Law.

The boy's life at home, in Russia, conforms with the religious education received at the *chaider*. On

*Going to the synagogue*

*Friday night prayer*

Friday afternoon, when the Sabbath begins, and on Saturday morning, when it continues, he is free from school, and on Friday does errands for his mother or helps in the preparation for the Sabbath. In the afternoon he commonly bathes, dresses freshly in Sabbath raiment, and goes to *chaider* in the evening. Returning from school, he finds his mother and sisters dressed in their best, ready to "greet the Sabbath." The lights are glowing in the candlesticks, the father enters with *Good Shabbas* on his lips, and is received by the grandparents, who occupy the seats of honor. They bless him and the children in turn. The father then chants the hymn of praise and salutation; a cup of wine or cider is passed from one to the other; every one washes his hands; all arrange themselves at table in the order of age, the youngest sitting at the father's right hand. After the meal they sing a song dedicated to the Sabbath and say grace. The same ceremony is repeated on Saturday morning, and afterward the children are examined in what they have learned of the holy Law during the week. The numerous religious holidays are observed in the same way, with special ceremonies of their own in addition. The important thing to notice is that the boy's whole training and education bear directly on ethics and religion, in the study of which he is encouraged to spend his whole life.

In a simple Jewish community in Russia, where the *chaider* is the only school, where the government is hostile and the Jews therefore thrown back upon their own customs, the boy loves his religion, he loves and honors his parents, his highest ambition is to be a great scholar—to know the Bible in all its glorious meaning, to know the Talmudical comments upon it, and to serve God. Above every one else he respects the aged, the Hebrew scholar, the rabbi, the teacher. Piety and wisdom count more than riches, talent, and power. The Law outweighs all else in value. Abraham and Moses, David and Solomon, the prophet Elijah, are the kind of great men to whom his imagination soars.

---

We were all Orthodox Jews on the Lower East Side of New York—and poor Orthodox Jews at that.

We heard vague rumors that the rich Jews uptown sat in temples without hats listening to organ music—but we did not believe it. To us the Sabbath was the most important holiday in our religion. Living on the Lower East Side during the first twenty years of this century was an experience few people can forget. And this experience centered around the Sabbath. The Irish and Italian boys had Christmas once a year; we had exaltation every Friday.

In the most populous neighborhood of the world, rent by the shouts of peddlers, the screams of children, and the myriad noises of the city, there was every Friday evening a wondrous stillness, an eloquent silence. So quiet was it that two blocks from the synagogue you could hear the muffled chant of the cantor and the murmured prayers of the congregation. Once the service was over, you came home to find your mother dressed in her wedding dress with a white silk scarf around her head. And your father told you all the sufferings throughout the centuries were dedicated for this moment, the celebration of the Sabbath.

In the Jewish household the father was a figure of authority, the boss. This meant that no one sat down to the dinner table until he came home from work and that we did not speak until he spoke first or until he had asked us a question. Jews call this *derekh eretz*—a phrase literally translated as "the custom of the land." In actual usage it means respect for elders and particularly for parents. My mother made all the decisions but she was always obedient to the idea of *derekh eretz*. Alone, she would tell my father: "I found a new apartment on Ludlow Street. I paid a deposit and I've asked the moving van to come Monday." That evening at the dinner table during a lull she would say: "Children, pay attention. Papa has something very important to say to you." Father would proceed to describe the move the next Monday, and Mother would listen as though hearing it for the first time, even congratulating him afterward on his excellent judgment.

The idea of *derekh eretz* was so deeply ingrained in the children that the most effective discipline within the family was The Look. If you forgot yourself and started roughhousing with your brothers, your father suddenly raised his head and gave you The Look. He simply stared at you as a warning of displeasure. It shamed you. You stopped. No words exchanged. Many a boy said he would rather submit to a whipping than suffer The Look from his father. Occasionally, however, Mother herself employed The Look, and against your father when she thought he was unfair. This too was silent communication. The mother stared at the father but her face had a new tension. She opened her eyes wide and raised her chin and, as articulate as any sentence, her look said, "Why don't you leave the kid alone?"

---

But in America, even before he begins to go to our public schools, the little Jewish boy finds himself in contact with a new world which stands in violent contrast with the Orthodox environment of his first few years. Insensibly—at the beginning—from his playmates in the streets, from his older brother or sister, he picks up a little English, a little American slang, hears older boys boast of prizefighter Bernstein, and learns vaguely to feel that there is a strange and fascinating life on the street. At this tender age he may even begin to black boots, gamble in pennies, and be filled with a "wild surmise" about American dollars.

With his entrance into the public school the little fellow runs plump against a system of education and a set of influences which are at total variance with those traditional to his race and with his home life.

The religious element is entirely lacking. The educational system of the public schools is heterogeneous and worldly. The boy becomes acquainted in the school reader with fragments of writings on all subjects, with a little mathematics, a little history. His instruction, in the interests of a liberal nonsectarianism, is entirely secular. English becomes his most familiar language. He achieves a growing comprehension and sympathy with the independent, free, rather skeptical spirit of the American boy; he rapidly imbibes ideas about social equality and contempt for authority, and tends to prefer Sherlock Holmes to Abraham as a hero.

---

No one knew in 1902 that the free public school would become the most important factor in the development of the Jewish community of America. But so it became probably because the free public school became as important a development to modern America itself. Not a day went by that we didn't see new immigrants walking down the middle of the street, each with a tag around the neck bearing a surname and with a piece of paper in hand, which was the address of a relative. And on the next Monday, the children of these immigrants enrolled in the public school. And it was the public school that proceeded to make citizens out of immigrants and do it within a single generation, surely the most successful endeavor in the history of personal relationships.

How long does it take to become an American?

We came from a little village in Eastern Europe in 1905, an eighteenth-century village in the province of Galicia, and four years later I was a "king" of my first-grade class, proudly marching beside my "queen" in New York's Hudson-Fulton Celebration of 1909.

We learned history and English. When a new greenhorn came to the class, frightened and confused, unable to manage any English, all knew that within six months he would be able to stand before us and, heavy accent and all, recite:

*I love the name of Washington,*
*I love my country, too.*
*I love the flag, the dear old flag,*
*The red, the white, the blue.*

This public-school system also provided many of us with an understanding of the Christian world, which heretofore had been a strange and forbidding world. The first Christians the younger Jews knew were the public-school teachers, far different from those Christians our parents muttered about who had populated Europe. These public-school teachers were sexless saints to most of us, and we fully believed they were unencumbered by the usual physical apparatus that slowed everyone else down. We considered these teachers the most wonderful people in the world, and it is surprising to remember the awe in which the Jewish community held them (How frightened our parents were when a teacher summoned them to school!) and then realize today it is the teacher, ironically, who is frightened of the parents.

In addition to the public schools, the libraries, and the fraternal *vereins,* a whole crop of private schools mushroomed on the Lower East Side. The Hebrew Technical Institute and the Baron de Hirsch School offered not only free textbooks but free shower baths. The shower bath was a symbol of luxury to the ghetto. The tenements were crowded in those days and few were equipped with bathtubs. The city provided public baths, and the Jewish women had their *mikva,* the ritual bath of purification after the menstrual period.

At the Hebrew Technical Institute, the charge for a shower bath was one cent a day, but that penny also included a lunch. Tuition was free. The applicant had to be sixteen years of age and prove he had some means of support while learning a trade. The school offered the following courses of instruction: plumbing and gas fitting, carpentry, house painting, sign painting, machinery, and electricity. The course of instruction lasted six months.

There was also a training school for girls founded by the Baroness de Hirsch. This school offered millinery, cooking, hand sewing—virtually the complementary trades the Hebrew Technical Institute and the Baron de Hirsch School taught boys. The baroness stipulated that at least ten per cent of the student body be Gentile girls.

Mr. Frank Damrosch, of the great musical family, founded the People's Singing Classes. This group was for working people who met in the evening after the workday was done. Forty or fifty people sat around listening to the records of great operas and then heard a lecture about the composer and the story line of the opera.

And, of course, business schools proliferated. There were dozens of business schools for girls, many of them conducted in the front room of a tenement. Immigrant mothers, chattering on the street, would boast, "My Clara is learning all three"; this meant that Clara was studying bookkeeping, typing, and stenography.

---

The Orthodox Jewish influences, still at work upon him, are rapidly weakened. He grows to look upon the ceremonial life at home as rather ridiculous. His old parents, who speak no English, he regards as greenhorns. English becomes his habitual tongue, even at home, and Yiddish he begins to forget. He still goes to *chaider*, but under conditions exceedingly different from those obtaining in Russia, where there are no public schools, and where the boy is consequently shut up within the confines of Hebraic education. In America the *chaider* assumes a position entirely subordinate. Compelled by law to go to the American public school, the boy can attend *chaider* only before the public school opens in the morning or after it closes in the afternoon. At such times the Hebrew teacher, who dresses in a long black coat, outlandish tall hat, and commonly speaks no English, visits the boy at home, or the boy goes to a neighboring *chaider*.

Contempt for the *chaider's* teaching comes the more easily because the boy rarely understands his Hebrew lessons to the full. His real language is English, the teacher's is commonly Yiddish, and the language to be learned is Hebrew. The problem before him is consequently the strangely difficult one of learning Hebrew, a tongue unknown to him, through a translation into Yiddish, a language of growing unfamiliarity, which, on account of its poor dialectic character, is an inadequate vehicle of thought.

---

I doubt seriously whether the immigrant boy thought of the *chaider* contemptuously. It was not contempt really. It was that other goals and interests crowded the *chaider*. Boys studying Hebrew today are restless in classes when the World Series comes around. I rather believe my attitudes, which concentrated on how to become an American, were the common attitudes. The *chaider* did not further these goals, and so I was impatient with it.

It is true that parents were saddened by this turn of events which watered down their Orthodoxy, but they were resigned to the fact that they couldn't have it both ways. The vast majority of the immigrants wanted their children to reflect the life and culture of America, and as quickly as possible.

There were mothers unable to speak a word of English who went to the branch library on Rivington Street and simply held up to the librarian a finger for each child. And the librarian issued cards, one for each finger. The mother went home and distributed the cards to her offspring and instructed them: "Go. Go and learn. Go now."

I have insisted that the public school was the greatest influence on the immigrant Jews. Next in importance was the library, followed by the settlement house and the clubs they fostered.

There were as many clubs on the Lower East Side as there were pushcarts and peddlers. There were debating clubs, political-study clubs, Zionist clubs, English clubs for older people learning the language, socialist clubs, dancing clubs, art clubs, and anarchist clubs. So many clubs were there that the New York City board of education used to keep the school buildings open at night to provide enough meeting places.

---

The Orthodox parents begin to see that the boy, in order to get along in the new world, must receive a Gentile training. Instead of hoping to make a rabbi of him, they reluctantly consent to his becoming an American businessman, or, still better, an American doctor or lawyer. The Hebrew teacher, less convinced of the usefulness and importance of his work, is in this country more simply commercial and less disinterested than abroad; a man generally, too, of less scholarship as well as of less devotion.

The growing sense of superiority on the part of the boy to the Hebraic part of his environment extends itself soon to the home. He learns to feel that his parents, too, are greenhorns. In the struggle between the two sets of influences that of the home becomes less and less effective. He runs away from the supper table to join his gang on the Bowery, where he is quick to pick up the very latest slang, where his talent for caricature is developed often at the expense of his parents, his race, and all foreigners; for he is an American, he is "the people," and like his glorious countrymen in general, he is quick to ridicule the stranger. He laughs at the foreign Jew with as much heartiness as at the Italian, for he feels that he himself is almost as remote from the one as from the other.

"Why don't you say your evening prayer, my son?" asks his mother in Yiddish.

"Ah, what yer givin' us!" replies, in English, the little American-Israelite as he makes a beeline for the street.

The boys not only talk together of picnics, of the crimes of which they read in the English newspapers, of prizefights, of budding business propositions, but they gradually quit going to synagogue, give up *chaider* promptly when they are thirteen years old, avoid the Yiddish theaters, seek the uptown places of amusement, dress in the latest American fashion, and have a keen eye for the right thing in neckties. They even refuse sometimes to be present at supper on Friday evenings. Then, indeed, the sway of the old people is broken.

*"Amerikane kinder, Amerikane kinder!"* wails the old father, shaking his head. The trend of things is

indeed too strong for the old man of the eternal Talmud and ceremony.

An important circumstance in helping to determine the boy's attitude toward his father is the tendency to reverse the ordinary and normal educational and economical relations existing between father and son. In Russia the father gives the son an education and supports him until his marriage, and often afterward, until the young man is able to take care of his wife and children. The father is, therefore, the head of the house in reality. But in the New World the boy contributes very early to the family's support. The father is in this country less able to make an economic place for himself than is the son. The little fellow sells papers, blacks boots, and becomes a street merchant on a small scale. As he speaks English, and his parents do not, he is commonly the interpreter in business transactions and tends generally to take things into his own hands. There is a tendency, therefore, for the father to respect the son.

There is many a huge building on Broadway which is the external sign (with the Hebrew name of the tenant emblazoned on some extended surface) of the energy and independence of some ignorant little Russian Jew, the son of a pushcart peddler or sweatshop worker, who began his business career on the sidewalks, selling newspapers, blacking boots, dealing in candles, shoestrings, fruit, etc., and continued it by peddling in New Jersey or on Long Island until he could open a small basement store on Hester Street, then a more extensive establishment on Canal Street—ending perhaps as a rich merchant on Broadway. The little fellow who starts out on this laborious climb is a model of industry and temperance. His only recreation, outside of business, which for him is a pleasure in itself, is to indulge in some simple pastime which generally is calculated to teach him something. On Friday or Saturday afternoon he is likely, for instance, to take a long walk to the park, where he is seen keenly inspecting the animals and perhaps boasting of his knowledge about them. He is an acquisitive little fellow, and seldom enjoys himself unless he feels that he is adding to his figurative or literal stock.

The cloak-and-umbrella business in New York is rapidly becoming monopolized by the Jews who began in the ghetto; and they are also very large clothing merchants. Higher, however, than a considerable merchant in the world of business, the little ghetto boy, born in a patriarchal Jewish home, has not yet attained. The Jews who as bankers, brokers, and speculators on Wall Street control millions never have been ghetto Jews. They came from Germany, where conditions are very different from those in Russia, Galicia, and Rumania, and where, through the comparatively liberal education of a secular character which they were able to obtain, they were already beginning to have a national life outside of the Jewish traditions. Then, too, these Jews who are now prominent in Wall Street have been in this country much longer than their Russian brethren. They are frequently the sons of Germans who in the last generation attained commercial rank. If they were born abroad, they came many years before the Russian immigration began and before the American ghetto existed, and have consequently become thoroughly identified with American life. Some of them began, indeed, as peddlers on a very small scale, traveled, as was more the habit with them then than now, all over the country, and rose by small degrees to the position of great financial operators. But they became so only by growing to feel very intimately the spirit of American enterprise, which enables a man to carry on the boldest operation in a calm spirit.

To this boldness the son of the Orthodox parents of our ghetto has not yet attained. Coming from the cramped quarter, with still a tinge of the patriarchal Jew in his blood, not yet thoroughly at home in the atmosphere of the American "plunger," he is a little hesitant, though very keen, in business affairs. The conservatism instilled in him by the pious old greenhorn, his father, is a limitation to his American nerve. He likes to deal in ponderable goods, to be able to touch and handle his wares, to have them before his eyes. In the next generation, when in business matters also he will be an instinctive American, he will become as big a financial speculator as any of them, but at present he is pretty well content with his growing business on Broadway and his fine residence uptown.

Although as compared with the American or German-Jewish financier who does not turn a hair at the gain or loss of a million, and who in personal manner maintains a phlegmatic, Napoleonic calm which is almost the most impressive thing in the world to an ordinary man, the young fellow of the ghetto seems a hesitant little dickerer. Yet, of course, he is a rising businessman, and, as compared to the world from which he has emerged, a very tremendous entity indeed. It is not strange, therefore, that this progressive merchant, while yet a child, acquires a self-sufficiency, and independence, and sometimes an arrogance which not unnaturally, at least in form, is extended even toward his parents.

If this boy were able entirely to forget his origin, to cast off the ethical and religious influences which are his birthright, there would be no serious struggle in his soul, and he would not represent a peculiar element in our society. He would be like any other practical, ambitious, rather worldly American boy. The struggle is strong because the boy's nature, at once religious and susceptible, is strongly appealed to by both the old and new. At the same time that he is keenly sensitive to the charm of his American environment, with its practical and national opportunities, he has still a deep love for his race and the old things. He is aware, and rather ashamed, of the limitations of his parents. He feels that the trend and weight of things are against them, that they are in a minority; but yet in a real way the old people remain his conscience, the visible representatives of a moral and religious tradition by which the boy may regulate his inner life.

The attitude of such a boy toward his father and mother is sympathetically described by Dr. Blaustein, principal of the Educational Alliance: "Not knowing that I speak Yiddish, the boy often acts as interpreter between me and his exclusively Yiddish-speaking father and mother. He always shows a great fear that I should be ashamed of his parents and tries to show them in the best light. When he translates, he expresses, in his manner, great affection and tenderness toward these people, whom he feels he is protecting; he not merely turns their Yiddish into good English, but modifies the substance of what they say in order to make them appear presentable, less outlandish and queer. He also manifests cleverness in translating for his parents what I say in English. When he finds that I can speak Yiddish and therefore can converse heart to heart with the old people, he is delighted. His face beams, and he expresses in every way that deep pleasure which a person takes in the satisfaction of honored protégés."

The third considerable influence in the life of the ghetto boy is that of the socialists.

---

Abraham Cahan, later to become editor of the *Vorwärts* (*Jewish Daily Forward*) and author of *The Rise of David Levinsky*, made the first socialist speech in Yiddish in August, 1882, in a hall behind a German saloon. He also printed the first Yiddish socialist handbills to recruit party members. The socialist movement on the Lower East Side was born out of the terror of the sweatshop. The first meaningful political action by the Jewish socialists came in the support of Henry George in his campaign for mayor in 1886. Later these groups became the nucleus of the United Hebrew Trades, established in 1888 as a federation of Yiddish-speaking locals. New trade unions in which Jewish workers predominated joined the nucleus soon.

The International Ladies' Garment Workers' Union was founded in 1900, followed by the Cap Makers' Union in 1901, the Fur Workers' Union in 1904, and the Amalgamated Clothing Workers' Union in 1914. The mass strikes of 1909-1914, known as the Great Revolt, and the 1911 Triangle Shirtwaist Factory fire, which took the lives of one hundred and forty-three girls, were the turning points in the history of the Jewish labor movement. The Great Revolt and the Triangle fire gave this movement an impetus which it never lost.

The first general strike in the needle trades began on November 22, 1909, when twenty thousand Jewish factory girls, makers of blouses and skirts, walked out. The city hummed Charles Harris' tune "Heaven Will Protect the Working Girl," as upper and middle-class women joined the picket lines after mounted police tried routing the strikers. For the first time uptown Gentile help came to the Lower East Side sweatshop workers. Christian clergymen and churchwomen from all over the city picketed with the shop girls.

The following year the entire garment industry was paralyzed by the city's biggest strike when sixty thousand cloakmakers put down their tools. Dismayed by the bitterness of the struggle between Jewish workers and Jewish employers, and by the use of Jewish thugs to assault strikers, the uptown Jewish community helped bring about a settlement. Louis Marshall and Jacob Schiff, with the aid of Louis D. Brandeis, who came down from Boston to serve as chairman of the mediation board that drafted "the protocol of peace," marked a milestone in the history of industrial relations. The settlement sounded the death knell of the sweatshop by abolishing piecework in the home and contractors' shops. It also gave the workers shorter hours, higher wages, and decent working conditions, and set a precedent for peaceful resolution of labor conflicts in other industries by creating a permanent arbitration machinery.

The Jewish unions also wielded important political influence in New York. As the backbone of the Socialist party, they elected Meyer London to the House of Representatives, seated several Socialists in the state legislature, and enabled Morris Hillquit to make a remarkable showing in the 1917 mayoralty election.

But soon the regular Democratic party organization began to make serious inroads, particularly among the children of the immigrants. Tammany Hall demonstrated beneficence to the voters of the Lower East Side, a beneficence expanded mostly to augment and increase the vested interest of the political leaders.

The reformers and the church people were just as eager to help, and for a less selfish reason, but they all lived "uptown," in what we considered fancy homes. They were remote and their help indirect. The Tammany fellow was "here."

The family in need of rent, coal, or food; the boy in trouble; the unmarried mother—none of these people had a place to go, even for advice, except to the Tammany clubhouse. At this level, the advice and performance were usually good. Often the Tammany fellow saved a family from disaster. The Tammany organization had a network of cooperating churches, priests, monasteries, Jewish organizations, and rabbis to whom it recommended boys and girls with special problems and it followed up to make sure situations were corrected or at least bettered.

And there was another factor—the need to be self-employed. The East Side boys knew that success in the professions came as a result of "contacts." Thus the law students joined the local Tammany Club or the Republican Club, and the political struggle began.

In 1912, William Howard Taft said that Jews "make the best Republicans," and forty years later Adlai Stevenson said that Jews "make the best Democrats."

It was not long before young East Side Jews participated in reform movements that had nothing to do with bettering their own conditions, except as it helped the city as a whole. They joined the uptown reformers. One of these early involvements in reform was in the political campaign of William Travers Jerome. Mr. Jerome ran for district attorney of New York against the Tammany machine. He made a campaign speech before an uptown audience that became the talk of the coffee houses along the East Side. Mr. Jerome was an aristocrat, a "blueblood," as members of the privileged classes were known in the first decade of the twentieth century. To an audience of these "bluebloods" he said: "You are of my own class. I was born and bred with you. But I want to say that you are of no use to this city. I feel bitterly against you because of your heartlessness. You are as bad as the people I am fighting in the lowliest dives of this city. You are too respectable to care about the teeming tenements and the hovels where crouch in darkness a million people of this city. It is you, the better people, who are responsible for the conditions of this city today. Do you think I want your vote? Take your votes to Tammany, that is where they belong. But remember this—the only civic and welfare work being done in this city today is being done by the Irish Catholic charities and Russian Jews on the Lower East Side of New York. Shame on you."

Mr. Jerome was elected and gave the brothels and the crooked politicians a bad time. Since most of the East Side press depended on Tammany for advertising support, none supported Jerome. The Jerome candidacy needed a campaign paper to reach the mass of Jewish voters, and the groups of Jewish reformers provided this support. A Mr. Fred Stein published ten weekly editions, each with a circulation of a hundred thousand, privately subsidized without advertising. This is an interesting episode in the history of American politics. When you see a four-page political tabloid during a race for the Senate or for a governorship, remember the first ever produced was called *William Travis Jerome* and was published in Yiddish in the ghetto of New York.

---

I am inclined to think that socialism is the least important and the least desirable of the three in its effect on his character.

Socialism as it is agitated in the Jewish quarter consists in a wholesale rejection, often founded on a misunderstanding, of both American and Hebraic ideals. The socialists harp monotonously on the relations between capital and labor, the injustice of classes, and assume literature to comprise one school alone, the Russian, at the bottom of which there is a strongly anarchistic and reactionary impulse. The son of a socialist laborer lives in a home where the main doctrines are two: that the old religion is rubbish and that American institutions were invented to exploit the workingman. The natural effects on such a boy are two: a tendency to reject the old implicit piety and to look with distrust at the genuinely American life about him.

The ideal situation for this young Jew would be that in which he could become an integral part of American life without losing the seriousness of nature developed by Hebraic tradition and education. At present he feels a conflict between these two influences: his youthful ardor and ambition lead him to prefer the progressive, if chaotic and uncentered, American life, but his conscience does not allow him entire peace in a situation which involves a chasm between him and his parents and their ideals. If he could find, along the line of his more exciting interests, the American, something that would fill the deeper need of his nature, his problem would receive a happy solution.

At present, however, the powers that make for the desired synthesis of the old and the new are fragmentary and unimportant. They consist largely in more or less charitable institutions such as the University Settlement, the Educational Alliance, and those free Hebrew schools which are carried on with definite reference to the boy as an American citizen. The free Hebrew schools differ from the *chaiders* in several respects. The important difference is that these schools are better organized, have better teachers, and have as a conscious end the supplementing of the boy's common-school education. The attempt is to add to the boy's secular training an ethical and religious training through the intelligent study of the Bible. It is thought that an acquaintance with the old literature of the Jews is calculated to deepen and spiritualize the boy's nature.

The Educational Alliance is a still better-organized and more intelligent institution, having much more the same purpose in view as the best Hebrew schools. Its avowed purpose is to combine the American and Hebrew elements, reconcile fathers and sons by making the former more American and the latter more Hebraic, and in that way improve the home life of the quarter. With the character of the University Settlement nearly everybody is familiar. It falls in line with Anglo-Saxon charitable institutions, forms classes, improves the condition of the poor, and acts as an ethical agent. But, though such institutions as the above may do a great deal of good, they are yet too fragmentary and external, are too little a vital growth from the conditions, to supply the demand for a serious life which at the same time shall be American.

---

Helping in the Americanization of the Jews was the Educational Alliance, opened in 1883 as the Y.M.H.A.'s downtown branch, then expanded by merging with the Hebrew Free School Association and the Hebrew Technical Institute. The Educational Alliance was the first settlement house in the United States. Its volunteer teachers included some of the city's most cultured Jews —among them Emma Lazarus, the poet; Oscar Straus, the diplomat; and Henry Leipziger, founder of the adult education system and first principal of the Alliance. Out of the Alliance's classes came a long line of eminent citizens. David Sarnoff, radio and TV tycoon, learned English there, and so did his British counterpart, Sir Louis Stirling. Eddie Cantor's career began as an amateur entertainer at the Alliance's summer camp, and at the Alliance hall, Arthur Murray learned to dance. Morris Raphael Cohen tested his ideas as a youthful Alliance orator. It was as a member of the Alliance that Sholom Aleichem wrote many of his works, lectured in the auditorium, and discussed literature and world Jewish themes with other members. Sir Jacob Epstein, Jo Davidson, Chaim Gross, William Auerbach-Levy, and Abraham Walkowitz paid three cents a lesson at the Alliance's art school. When Epstein was knighted, having become a British subject in 1912, Walkowitz said to the sculptor's brother, "I see Jake is Sir Jake now." "Pfui," retorted the brother. "Jake was knighted at 102 Hester Street." Which is where Epstein had found his first models among pushcart peddlers.

The bad housing, health, and social conditions on

the Lower East Side after 1880 impelled dedicated reformers to establish the Henry Street Settlement, the University Settlement, the College Settlement, the Clark House, the Christadora House, and the Madison House. In the settlement house on Henry Street, founded by Lillian Wald, and in other East Side settlements, uptown Jewish volunteers introduced practical social welfare and developed some of the liberal concepts that were later converted into legislation by Al Smith, F.D.R., Robert Wagner, and Herbert H. Lehman. In these islands of hope, Lehman, Henry Morgenthau, Jr., Belle Moskowitz, Gerard Swope, and Joseph Proskauer worked side by side with Eleanor Roosevelt, Frances Perkins, Adolph Berle, and Harry Hopkins in the battle for housing, reform, parks, playgrounds, cleaner streets, and public health services.

I attended the University Settlement on Rivington and Eldridge streets. I remember Eleanor Roosevelt, a tall, thin woman in black ribbed bicycle stockings and blue bloomers. Little Jewish girls attended her dancing class.

---

But the ghetto boy is making use of his heterogeneous opportunities with the greatest energy and ambition. The public schools are filled with little Jews; the night schools of the East Side are used by practically no other race. City College, New York University, and Columbia University are graduating Russian Jews in numbers rapidly increasing. Many lawyers, indeed, children of patriarchal Jews, have very large practices already, and some of them belong to solid firms on Wall Street, although as to business and financial matters they have not yet attained to the most spectacular height. Then there are innumerable boys' debating clubs, ethical clubs, and literary clubs in the East Side. Altogether there is an excitement in ideas and an enthusiastic energy for acquiring knowledge which has interesting analogy to the hopefulness and acquisitive desire of the early Renaissance. It is a mistake to think that the young Hebrew turns naturally to trade. He turns his energy to whatever offers the best opportunities for broader life and success. Other things besides business are open to him in this country, and he is improving his chance for the higher education as devotedly as he has improved his opportunities for success in business.

It is easy to see that the ghetto boy's growing Americanism will be easily triumphant at once over the old traditions and the new socialism. Whether or not he will be able to retain his moral earnestness and native idealism will depend not so much upon him as upon the development of American life as a whole. What we need at the present time more than anything else is a spiritual unity such as, perhaps, will only be the distant result of our present special activities. We need something similar to the spirit underlying the national and religious unity of the Orthodox Jewish culture.

Although the young men of the ghetto who represent at once the most intelligent and the most progressively American are, for the most part, floundering about without being able to find the social growths upon which they can rest as true Americans while retaining their spiritual and religious earnestness, there are yet a small number of them who have already attained a synthesis not lacking in the ideal. I know a young artist, a boy born in the ghetto, who began his conscious American life with contempt for the old things, but who with growing culture has learned to perceive the beauty of the traditions and faith of his race. He puts into his paintings of the types of Hester Street an imaginative, almost religious, idealism, and his artistic sympathy seems to extend particularly to the old people. He, for one, has become reconciled to the spirit of his father without ceasing to be an American. And he is not alone. There are other young Jews, of American university education, of strong ethical and spiritual character, who are devoting themselves to the work of forming, among the boys of the ghetto, an ideal at once American and consistent with the spirit at the heart of the Hebraic tradition.

## THE INTELLECTUALS

Between the old people, with their religion, their traditions, the life pointing to the past, and the boy with his young life eagerly absorbent of the new tendencies, is a third class, the members of which may be called the intellectuals of the ghetto. This is the most picturesque and interesting, although not the most permanently significant, of all. The members of this class are interesting for what they are rather than for what they have been or for what they may become. They are the anarchists, the socialists, the editors, the writers, some of the scholars, poets, playwrights, and actors of the quarter. They are the "enlightened" ones who are at once neither Orthodox Jews nor Americans. Coming from Russia, they are reactionary in their political opinions, and in matters of taste and literary ideals are Europeans rather than Americans. When they die they will leave nothing behind them; but while they live they include the most educated, forcible, and talented personalities of the quarter. Most of them are socialists, and, as I pointed out in the last section, socialism is not a permanently nutritive element in the life of the ghetto, for as yet the ghetto has not learned to know the conditions necessary to American life, and cannot, therefore, effectively react against them.

It is this class which contains, however, the many men of ideas who bring about in certain circles a veritable intellectual fermentation, and are therefore most interesting from what might be called a literary point of view, as well as of great importance in the education of the people. Gifted Russian Jews hold forth passionately to crowds of workingmen; devoted writers exploit in the Yiddish newspapers the principles of their creed and take violent part in the labor agitation of the East Side or produce realistic sketches of the life in the quarter, underlying which can be felt the same kind of revolt which is apparent in the analogous literature of Russia. The intellectual excitement in the air causes many splits among the socialists. They gather in hostile camps, run rival organs; each prominent man has his "patriots"—the faithful adherents who support him right or wrong. Intense personal abuse and the most violent denunciation of opposing principles are the rule. Mellowness, complacency, geniality, and calmness are qualities practically unknown to the intellectual Russian Jews, who, driven from the old country, now possess the first opportunity to express themselves. On the other hand they are free of the stupid Philistinism of content and are not primarily interested in the dollar. Their poets sing pathetically of the sweatshops, of universal brotherhood, of the abstract rights of man. Their enthusiastic young men gather every evening in cafés of the quarter and become habitually intoxicated with the excitement of ideas. In their restless and feverish eyes shines the intense idealism of the combined Jew and Russian—the moral earnestness of the Hebrew united with the passionate, rebellious mental activity of the modern Muscovite. In these cafés they meet after the theater or an evening lecture and talk into the morning hours. The ideal, indeed, is alive within them. The defect of their intellectual ideas is that they are not founded on historical knowledge, or on knowledge of the conditions with which they have to cope. In their excitement and extremeness they resemble the spirit on the French intellectuals of 1789 rather than that more conservative feeling which has always directed the development of Anglo-Saxon communities.

Among the intellectuals may be classed a certain number of poets, dramatists, musicians, and writers, who are neither socialists nor anarchists, constituting what might roughly be called the literary bohemia of the quarter—men who pursue their art for the love of it simply, or who are thereto impelled by the necessity of making a precarious living, men real-

Jacob Epstein caught the idea and spirit in his sketches of the coffee houses and the new woman who visited them. For this drawing his model may have been an unmarried factory worker who read books all the time. Perhaps she lived in a dreary, dingy hall bedroom, a boarder in a slum tenement flat, with a family of a father, a mother, and five children. She spent as much time as she could in the bright cheery atmosphere of the coffee house. She was rarely the recipient of courtesies, but then she never missed courtesies, never having known too many. But there was one gesture shown her. In a heated argument, her opponent invariably refrained from cracking her over the head with a rolled-up newspaper!

ly without ideas in the definite, belligerent sense, often uneducated, but often of considerable native talent. There are also many men of brains who form a large professional class—doctors, lawyers, and dentists—and who yet are too old when they come to America to be thoroughly identified with the life. They are, however, a useful part of the Jewish community, and, like others of the intellectual class, are often men of great devotion, who have left comparative honor and comfort in the old country in order to live and work with the persecuted or otherwise less fortunate brethren.

The greater number of the following chapters deal with the men of this intellectual class—their personalities, their literary work, and the light it throws upon the life of the people in the New York ghetto.

---

When the immigrants moved out of a neighborhood, they took their religious schools and their newspapers and their stores with them. But the places where they played remained. There were still a few Irish saloons and German beer gardens on the Lower East Side, which were now completely surrounded by Jewish coffee houses.

Though called a coffee house, most of them were places where the immigrant Jews drank tea and talked— and they talked as no other group has ever talked. They talked about Karl Marx and Bakunin, Henry George and Eugene Debs and Big Tim Sullivan. They talked about Ibsen and Dostoevsky and Shakespeare and Hegel. They talked about the performance of the prima donna at the Metroplitan Opera the night before. There were others whose whole day was a succession of tea and socialism. Still others denounced those who criticized the latest performance of the actor Jacob Adler, and wrote lengthy duel challenges to those who had traduced the playwright Jacob Gordin. All these topics were handled best over tea à la Russe, tea with a slice of lemon sipped between a sugar cube clenched in the teeth.

There were at least three hundred of these coffee houses on the Lower East Side, all of them daily populated.

# PROPHETS WITHOUT HONOR

A ragged man, who looks like a peddler or a beggar, picking his way through the crowded misery of Hester Street, or ascending the stairs of one of the dingy tenement houses full of sweatshops that line that busy mart of the poor ghetto Jew, may be a great Hebrew scholar. He may be able to speak and write the ancient tongue with the facility of a modern language—as fluently as the ordinary Jew makes use of the Yiddish of the people; he may be a manifold author with a deep and pious love for the beautiful poetry in his literature; in character he may be an enthusiast, a dreamer, or a good and reverend old man. But no matter what his attainments and his quality he is unknown and unhonored, for he has pinned his faith to a declining cause, writes his passionate accents in a tongue more and more unknown even to the cultivated Jew. Consequently, amid the crowding and material interests of the new world, he is submerged—poor in physical estate, his moral capital unrecognized by the people among whom he lives.

Not only unrecognized by the ignorant and the busy (and their teachers the rabbis, who in New

York are frequently nearly as ignorant as the people), he is also (as his learning is limited largely to the literature of his race) looked down upon by the influential and intellectual element of the ghetto— an element socialistic, in literary sympathy Russian rather than Hebraic, intolerant of everything not violently modern, wedded to "movements," and scornful of the past. The *maskil* (the man of wisdom, the Hebrew scholar), therefore, is called old fogy or dilettante, by the up-to-date socialists.

*Unknown and unhonored*

Of such men there are several in the humble corners of the New York ghetto. One peddles for a living, another has a printing office in a basement on Canal Street, a third occasionally tutors in some one of many languages and sells a patent medicine, and

*Moses Reicherson*

a fourth is the principal of the Talmud-Thora, a Hebrew school in the Harlem ghetto, where he teaches the children to read, and pray in the Hebrew language.

Moses Reicherson is the name of the principal. "Man of wisdom" of the purest kind, probably the finest Hebrew grammarian in New York, and one of the finest in the world, his income from his position at the head of the school is five dollars a week. He is seventy-three years old, wears a thick gray beard, a little cap on his head, and a long black coat. His wife is old and bent. They are alone in their miserable little apartment on East 106th Street. Their son died a year or two ago, and to cover the funeral expenses Mr. Reicherson tried in vain to sell his *Encyclopaedia Britannica*. But, nevertheless, the old scholar, who had been bending over his closely written manuscript, received the visitor with almost cheerful politeness and told the story of his work and of his ambitions. Of his difficulties and privations he said little, but they shone through his words and in the character of the room in which he lived.

Born in Vilnyus (sometimes called the Jerusalem of Lithuania or the Athens of modern Judea because of the number of enlightened Jews who have been born there, many of whom now live in the Russian-Jewish quarter of New York), he has retained the faith of his Orthodox parents, a faith, however, springing from the pure origin of Judaism rather than holding to the hair-splitting distinctions later embodied in the Talmud. He was a teacher of Hebrew in his native town for many years, where he stayed until he came to New York some years ago to be near his son. His two great intellectual interests, subordinated indeed to the love of the old literature and religion, have been Hebrew grammar and the moral fables of several languages. On the former he has written an important work, and of the latter has translated much of Lessing's and Gellert's work into pure Hebrew. He has also translated into his favorite tongue the Russian fable writer Krilow, has written fables of his own, and a Hebrew commentary on the Bible in twenty-four volumes. He loves the fables "because they teach the people and are real criticism—they are profound and combine fancy and thought." Many of these are still in manuscript, which is characteristic of much of the work of these scholars, for they have no money, and publishers do not run after Hebrew books. Also unpublished, written in lovingly minute characters, he has a Hebrew prayer book in many volumes. He has written hundreds of articles for the Hebrew weeklies and monthlies, which are fairly numerous in this country, but which seldom can afford to pay their contributors. At present he writes exclusively for a Hebrew weekly published in Chicago, *Regeneration,* the object of which is to promote "the knowledge of the ancient Hebrew language and literature, and to regenerate the spirit of the nation." For this he receives no pay, the editor being almost as poor as himself. But he writes willingly for the love of the cause, "for universal good," for Reicherson, in common with the other neglected scholars, is deeply interested in revivifying what is now among American Jews a dead language. He believes that in this way only can the Jewish people be taught the good and the true.

"When the national language and literature live," he said, "the nation lives; when dead, so is the nation. The holy tongue in which the Bible was written must not die. If it should, much of the truth of the Bible, many of its spiritual secrets, much of its beautiful poetry, would be lost. I have gone deep into the Bible, that greatest book, all my life, and I know many of its secrets." He beamed with pride as he said these words, and his sense of the beauty of the Hebrew spirit and the Hebrew literature led him to speak wonderingly of anti-Semitism. This cause seemed to him to be founded on ignorance of the Bible. "If the anti-Semites would only study the Bible, would go deep into the knowledge of Hebrew and the teaching of Christ, then everything would be sweet and well. If they would spend a little of that money in supporting the Hebrew language and literature and explaining the sacred books, which they now use against our race, they would see that they are anti-Christians rather than anti-Semites."

The scholar here bethought himself of an old fable he had translated into Hebrew. Cold and Warmth make a wager that the traveler will unwrap his cloak sooner to one than to the other. The fierce wind tries its best, but at every bold blast the traveler only wraps his cloak the closer. But when the sun throws its rays the wayfarer gratefully opens his breast to the warming beams. "Love solves all things," said the old man, "and hate closes up the channels to knowledge and virtue." Believing the Pope to be a good man with a knowledge of the Bible, he wanted to write him about the anti-Semites, but desisted on the reflection that the Pope was very old and overburdened, and that the letter would probably fall into the hands of the cardinals.

All this was sweetly said, for about him there was nothing of the attitude of complaint. His wife once or twice during the interview touched upon their personal condition, but her husband severely kept his mind on the universal truths, and only when questioned admitted that he would like a little more money, in order to publish his books and to enable him to think with more concentration about the Hebrew language and literature. There was no bitterness in his reference to the neglect of Hebrew scholarship in the ghetto. His interest was impersonal and detached, and his regret at the decadence of the language seemed noble and disinterested, and, unlike some of the other scholars, the touch of warm humanity was in everything he said. Indeed, he is rather the learned teacher of the people with deep religious and ethical sense than the scholar who cares only for learning. "In the name of God, adieu!" he said, with quiet intensity when the visitor withdrew.

Contrasting sharply in many respects with this beautiful old teacher is the man who peddles from tenement house to tenement house in the downtown ghetto to support himself and his three young children. S. B. Schwartzberg, unlike most of the submerged scholars, is still a young man, only thirty-seven years old, but he is already discouraged, bitter, and discontented. He feels himself the apostle of a lost cause—the regeneration in New York of the old Hebrew language and literature. His great enterprise in life has failed. He has now given it up, and the natural vividness and intensity of his nature get satisfaction in the strenuous abuse of the Jews of the ghetto.

He was born in Warsaw, Poland, the son of a distinguished rabbi. In common with many Russian and Polish Jews, he early obtained a living knowledge of the Hebrew language, and a great love of the literature, which he knows thoroughly, although unlike Reicherson and a scholar who is to be mentioned, Rosenberg, he has not contributed to the literature in a scientific sense. He is slightly bald, with burning black eyes, an enthusiastic and excited manner, and talks with almost painful earnestness.

Three years ago Schwartzberg came to this country with a great idea in his head. "In this free country," he thought to himself, "where there are so many Russian and Polish Jews, it is a pity that our tongue is dying, is falling into decay, and that the literature and traditions that hold our race together are being undermined by materialism and ethical skepticism." He had a little money, and he decided he would establish a journal in the interests of the Hebrew language and literature. No laws would prevent him here from speaking his mind in his beloved tongue. He would bring into vivid being again the national spirit of his people, make them love with the old fervor their ancient traditions and language. It was the race's spirit of humanity and feeling for the ethical beauty, not the special creed of Judaism, for which he and the other scholars care little, that filled him with the enthusiasm of an apostle. In his monthly magazine, the *Western Light,* he put his best efforts, his best thoughts about ethical truths and literature. The poet Dolitzki contributed in purest Hebrew verse, as did many ghetto lights. But it received no support, few bought it, and it lasted only a year. Then he gave it up, bankrupt in money and hope. That was several years ago, and since then he has peddled for a living.

The failure has left in Schwartzberg's soul a passionate hatred of what he calls the materialism of the Jews in America. Only in Europe, he thinks, does the love of the spiritual remain with them. Of the rabbis of the ghetto he spoke with bitterness. "They," he said, "are the natural teachers of the people. They could do much for the Hebrew literature and language. Why don't they? Because they know no Hebrew and have no culture. In Russia the Jews demand that their rabbis should be learned and spiritual, but here they are ignorant and materialistic." So Mr. Schwartzberg wrote a pamphlet which is now famous in the ghetto. "I wrote it with my heart's blood," he said, his eyes snapping. "In it I painted the spiritual condition of the Jews in New York in the gloomiest of colors."

"It is terrible," he proceeded vehemently. "Not one Hebrew magazine can exist in this country. They all fail, and yet there are many beautiful Hebrew writers today. When Dolitzki was twenty years old in Russia, he was looked up to as a great poet. But what do the Jews care about him here? For he writes in Hebrew! Why, Hebrew scholars are regarded by the Jews as tramps, as useless beings. Driven from Russia because we are Jews, we are despised in New York because we are Hebrew scholars! The rabbis, too, despise the learned Hebrew, and they have a fearful influence on the ignorant people. If they can dress well and speak English it is all they want. It is a shame how low-minded these teachers of the people are. I was born of a rabbi, and brought up by him, but in Russia they are for literature and the spirit, while in America it is just the other way."

The discouraged apostle of Hebrew literature now sees no immediate hope for the cause. What seems to him the most beautiful lyric poetry in the world he thinks doomed to the imperfect understanding of generations for whom the language does not live. The only ultimate hope is in the New Jerusalem. Consequently the fiery scholar, although not a Zion-

*Reverend H. Rosenberg*

ist, thinks well of the movement as tending to bring the Jews again into a nation which shall revive the old tongue and traditions. Mr. Schwartzberg referred to some of the other submerged scholars of the ghetto. His eyes burned with indignation when he spoke of Moses Reicherson. He could hardly control himself at the thought that the greatest Hebrew grammarian living—"an old man, too, a reverend old man"—should be brought to such a pass. In the same strain of outrage he referred to another old man, a scholar who would be as poor as Reicherson and himself were it not for his wife, who is a dressmaker. It is she who keeps him out of the category of submerged scholars.

But the Reverend H. Rosenberg, of whose condition Schwartzberg also bitterly complained, is indeed submerged. He runs a printing office in a Canal Street basement, where he sits in the damp all day long, waiting for an opportunity to publish his magnum opus, a cyclopedia of biblical literature, containing a historical and geographical description of the persons, places, and objects mentioned in the Bible. All the ghetto scholars speak of this work with bated breath, as a tremendously learned affair. Only two volumes of it have been published. To give the remainder to the world, Mr. Rosenberg is waiting for his children, who are nearly self-supporting, to contribute their mite. He is a man of sixty-two, with the high, bald forehead of a scholar. For twenty years he was a rabbi in Russia, and has preached in thirteen synagogues. He has been nine years in New York, and, in addition to the great cyclopedia, has written, but not published, a cyclopedia of Talmudical literature. A history of the Jews, in the Russian language, and a Russian novel, *The Jew of Trient,* are among his published works. He is one of the most learned of all of these men who have a living, as well as an exact, knowledge of what is generally regarded as a dead language and literature.

Although he is waiting to publish the great cyclopedia, he is patient and cold. He has not the sweet enthusiasm of Reicherson, and not the vehement and partisan passion of Schwartzberg. He has the coldness of old age without its spiritual glow, and scholarship is the only idea that moves him. Against the rabbis he has no complaint to make; with them, he said, he had nothing to do. He thinks that Schwartzberg is extreme and unfair, and that there are good and bad rabbis in New York. He is reserved and undemonstrative, and speaks only in reply. When the rather puzzled visitor asked him if there was anything in which he was interested, he replied, "Yes, in my cyclopedia." The only point at which he betrayed feeling was when he quoted proudly the words of a reviewer of the cyclopedia, who had wondered where Dr. Rosenberg had obtained all his learning. He stated indifferently that the Hebrew language and literature is dead and cannot be revived. "I know," he said, "that Hebrew literature does not pay, but I cannot stop." With no indignation, he remarked that the Jews in New York have no ideals. It was a fact objectively to be deplored, but for which he personally had no emotion, all of that being reserved for his cyclopedia.

These three men are perfect types of the submerged Hebrew scholar of the New York ghetto. Reicherson is the typical religious teacher; Schwartzberg, the enthusiast, who loves the language like a mistress; and Rosenberg, the cool "man of wisdom," who only cares for the perfection of knowledge. Although there are several others on the East Side who approach the type, they fall more or less short of it. Either they are not really scholars in the old tongue, although reading and even writing it, or through business or otherwise they have raised themselves above the pathetic point. Thus Dr. Benedict Ben-Zion, one of the poorest of all, being reduced to occasional tutoring, and the sale of a patent medicine for a living, is not specifically a scholar. He writes and reads Hebrew, to be sure, but is also a playwright in Yiddish, a doctor for many years, a teacher in several languages, one who has turned his hand to everything, and whose heart and mind are not so purely Hebraic as those of the men I have mentioned. He even is seen, more or less, with ghetto literati, who are essentially hostile to what the true Hebrew scholar holds by—a body of Russian-Jewish socialists of education, who in their Grand and Canal street cafés express every night in impassioned language their contempt for whatever is old and historical.

Then, there are: J. D. Eisenstein, the youngest and one of the most learned, but perhaps the least sub-

*Submerged scholars*

merged of them all; Gerson Rosenschweig, a wit, who has collected the epigrams of the Hebrew literature, added many of his own, and written in Hebrew a humorous treatise on America—(a very up-to-date Jew who, like Schwartzberg, tried to run a Hebrew weekly, but when he failed, was not discouraged, and turned to business and politics instead); and Joseph Low Sossnitz, a very learned scholar, of dry and sarcastic tendency, who only recently has risen above the submerged point. Among the latter's most notable published books are a philosophical attack on materialism, a treatise on the sun, and a work on the philosophy of religion.

It is the wrench between the past and the present which has placed these few scholars in their present pathetic condition. Most of them are old, and when they die the *maskil* as a type will have vanished from New York. In the meantime, though they starve, they must devote themselves to the old language, the old ideas and traditions of culture. Their poet, the austere Dolitzki, famous in Russia at the time of the revival of Hebrew twenty years ago, is the only man in New York who symbolizes in living verse the spirit in which these old men live, the spirit of love for the race as most purely expressed in the Hebrew literature. This disinterested love for the remote, this pathetic passion to keep the dead alive, is what lends to the lives of these submerged scholars a nobler quality than what is generally associated with the East Side.

The rabbis, as well as the scholars, of the East Side of New York have their grievances. They, too, are "submerged," like so much in humanity that is at once intelligent, poor and out of date. As a lot, they are old, reverent men, with long gray beards, long black coats, and little black caps on their heads. They are mainly very poor, live in the barest of the tenement houses, and pursue a calling which no longer involves much honor or standing. In the old country, in Russia—for most of the poor ones are Russian—the rabbi is a great person. He is made rabbi by the state and is rabbi all his life, and the only rabbi in the town, for all the Jews in every city form one congretation, of which there is but one rabbi and one cantor. He is a man always full of learning and piety, and is respected and supported comfortably by the congregation, a tax being laid on meat, salt, and other foodstuffs for his special bene-fit.

But in New York it is very different. Here there are hundreds of congregations, one on almost every street, for the Jews come from many different cities and towns in the old country, and the New York representatives of every little place in Russia must have their congregation here. Consequently, the congregations are for the most part small, poor, and unimportant. Few can pay the rabbi more than three or four dollars a week, and often, instead of having a regular salary, he is reduced to occasional fees for his services at weddings, births, and holy festivals generally. Some very poor congregations get along without a rabbi at all, hiring one for special occasions, but these are congregations which are falling off somewhat from their Orthodox strictness.

The result of this state of affairs is a pretty general falling-off in the character of the rabbis. In Russia they are learned men, know the Talmud and all the commentaries upon it by heart, and have degrees from the rabbinical colleges; but here they are often without degrees, frequently know comparatively little about the Talmud, and are sometimes actuated by worldly motives. A few Jews coming to New York from some small Russian town, will often select for a rabbi the man among them who knows a little more of the Talmud than the others, whether he has ever studied for the calling or not. Then, again, some mere adventurers get into the position—men good for nothing, looking for a position. They clap a high hat on their heads, impose on a poor congregation with their up-to-dateness, and become rabbis without learning or piety. These "fake" rabbis—"rabbis for business only"—are often satirized in the Yiddish plays given at the Bowery theaters. On the stage they are ridiculous figures, ape American manners in bad accents, and have a keen eye for gain.

The genuine, pious rabbis in the New York ghetto feel, consequently, that they have their grievances. They, the accomplished interpreters of the Jewish law, are well-nigh submerged by the frauds that flood the city. But this is not the only sorrow of the "real" rabbi of the ghetto. The rabbis uptown, the rich rabbis, pay little attention to the sufferings, moral and

*Rabbis for business only*

physical, of their downtown brethren. For the most
part the uptown rabbi is of the German, the downtown rabbi of the Russian branch of the Jewish race,
and these two divisions of the Hebrews hate one another like poison. Last winter, when Zangwill's
dramatized *The Children of the Ghetto* was produced
in New York, the periodicals of the swell uptown
German Jew protested that it was a pity to represent
faithfully in art the sordidness as well as the beauty
of the poor Russian ghetto Jew. It seemed particularly baneful that the religious customs of the Jews
should be thus detailed upon the stage. The uptown
Jew felt a little ashamed that the proletarians of his
people should be made the subject of literature. The
downtown Jews, the Russian Jews, however, received

plays and stories with delight, as expressing truth-fully their life and character, of which they are not ashamed.

Another cause of irritation between the downtown and uptown rabbis is a difference of religion. The up-town rabbi, representing congregations larger in this country and more American in comfort and tend-ency, generally is of the Reformed complexion, a hateful thought to the Orthodox downtown rabbi, who is loath to admit that the term rabbi fits these swell German "preachers." He maintains that, since the uptown rabbi is, as a rule, not only Reformed in faith, but in preaching as well, he is in reality no rabbi, for, properly speaking, a rabbi is simply an in-terpreter of the law, one with whom the Talmudical wisdom rests, and who alone can give it out—not one who exhorts, but who, on application, can untie knotty points of the Law. The uptown rabbis they call "preachers," with some disdain.

So that the poor, downtrodden rabbis—those among them who look upon themselves as the only genuine—have many annoyances to bear. Despised and neglected by their rich brethren, without honor or support in their own poor communities, and sur-rounded by a rabble of unworthy rivals, the "real" in-terpreter of the Law in New York is something of an object of pity.

Just who the most genuine downtown rabbis are is, no doubt, a matter of dispute. I will not attempt to determine, but will quote in substance a statement of Rabbi Weiss as to genuine rabbis, which will include a curious section of the history of the ghetto. He is a

*The rabbi declares it kosher*

jolly old man, and smokes his pipe in a tenement house room containing two hundred books of the Talmud and allied writings.

"A genuine rabbi," he said, "knows the Law, and sits most of the time in his room, ready to impart it. If an old woman comes in with a goose that has been killed, the rabbi can tell her, after she has explained how the animal met its death, whether or not it is *kosher*, whether it may be eaten or not. And on any other point of diet or general moral or physical hygiene the rabbi is ready to explain the Law of the Hebrews from the time of Adam until today. It is he who settles many of the quarrels of the neighborhood. The poor sweatshop Jew comes to complain of his boss, the old woman to tell him her dreams and get his interpretation on them, the young girl to weigh with him questions of amorous etiquette. Our children do not need to go to the Yiddish theaters to learn about greenhorn types. They see all sorts of ghetto Jews in the house of the rabbi, their father.

"I myself was the first genuine rabbi on the East Side of New York. I am now sixty-two years old, and came here sixteen years ago—came for pleasure, but my wife followed me, and so I had to stay."

Here the old rabbi smiled cheerfully. "When I came to New York," he proceeded, "I found the Jews here in a very bad way—eating meat that was *thrapho*—not allowed, because killed improperly, literally, killed by a brute. The slaughterhouses at that time had no rabbi to see that the meat was properly killed, was *kosher*—all right.

"You can imagine my horror. The slaughterhouses

had been employing an Orthodox Jew who, however, was not a rabbi, to see that the meat was properly killed, and he had been doing things all wrong, and the chosen people had been living abominably. I immediately explained the proper way of killing meat, and since then I have regulated several slaughter-houses and make my living in that way. I am also rabbi of a congregation, but it is so small that it doesn't pay. The slaughterhouses are more profitable."

These submerged rabbis are not always quite fair to one another. Some East Side authorities maintain that the "Orthodox Jew"—of whom Rabbi Weiss spoke thus contemptuously—was one of the finest rabbis who ever came to New York, one of the most erudite of Talmudic scholars. Many congregations united to call him to America in 1887, so great was his renown in Russia. But when he reached New York the general fate of the intelligent adult immigrant overtook him. Even the Orthodox in New York looked upon him as a greenhorn and deemed his sermons out of date. He was inclined, too, to insist upon a stricter observance of the Law than suited their lax American ideas. So he, too, famous in Russia, rapidly became one of the submerged.

One of the most learned, dignified, and impressive rabbis of the East Side is Rabbi Vidrovitch. He was a rabbi for forty years in Russia and for nine years in New York. Like all true rabbis, he does not preach, but merely sits in his home and expounds the Law. He employs the Socratic method of instruction, and is very keen in his indirect mode of argument. Keenness, indeed, seems to be the general result of the hair-splitting rabbinical education. The uptown rabbis—"preachers," as the downtown rabbi contemptuously calls them—send many letters to Rabbi Vidrovitch seeking his help in the untying of knotty points of the Law. It was from him that Israel Zangwill, when *The Children of the Ghetto* was produced on the New York stage, obtained a minute description of the Orthodox marriage ceremonies. Zangwill caused to be taken several flashlight photographs of the old rabbi, surrounded by his books and dressed in his official garments.

There are many congregations in the New York ghetto which have no rabbis and many rabbis who have no congregations. Two rabbis who have no congregations are Rabbi Beinush and Rabbi, or rather Cantor, Weiss. Rabbi Weiss would say of Rabbi Beinush that he is a man who knows the Talmud, but has no diploma. Rabbi Beinush is an extremely poor rabbi with neither congregation nor slaughterhouses, who sits in his poor room and occasionally sells his wisdom to a fishwife who wants to know if some piece of meat is *kosher* or not. He is down on the rich uptown rabbis, who care nothing for the Law, as he puts it, and who leave the poor downtown rabbi to starve.

Cantor Weiss is also without a job. The duty of the cantor is to sing the prayer in the congregation, but Cantor Weiss sings only on holidays, for he is not paid enough, he says, to work regularly, the cantor sharing in this country a fate similar to that of the rabbi. The famous comedian of the ghetto, Mogolesco, was, as a boy, one of the most noted cantors in Russia. As an actor in the New York ghetto he makes twenty times as much money as the most accomplished cantor here. Cantor Weiss is very bitter against the uptown cantors: "They shorten the prayer," he said. "They are not Orthodox. It is too hot in the synagogue for the comfortable uptown cantors to pray."

---

Orthodox Jews often traveled many miles to hear a *chazan*. During the High Holy Days the great cantors of the world visited New York City, and I remember when the cantor Sirota filled Hunt's Point Palace in The Bronx, a seating capacity of four thousand.

It was not unusual for the cantors to be applauded because of the emotion they aroused in the synagogue. One of the greatest European cantors, Kwartin, used to get an ovation when he entered the synagogue. In some synagogues rabbis posted watchmen to keep the people from leaving after the cantor was through. The decline of the cantor set in with the advent of English-speaking rabbis. The rabbis kept cutting the Hebrew liturgy, which most people didn't understand. Gradually the rabbi replaced the cantor as the dominant figure in the *shul*.

---

Comfortable Philistinism, progress, and enlightment uptown; poverty, Orthodoxy, and patriotic and religious sentiment, with a touch of the material also, downtown. Such seems to be the difference between the German and the Russian Jew in this country, and in particular between the German- and Russian-Jewish rabbi.

# three

# THE OLD AND NEW WOMAN

The women present in many respects a marked contrast to their American sisters. Substance as opposed to form, simplicity of mood as opposed to capriciousness, seem to be in broad lines their relative qualities. They have comparatively few *états d'âme;* but those few are revealed with directness and passion. They lack the subtle charm of the American woman, who is full of feminine devices, complicated flirtatiousness, who in her dress and personal appearance seeks the plastic epigram, and in her talk and relation to the world an indirect suggestive delicacy. They are poor in physical estate; many work or have worked; even the comparatively educated among them, in the sweatshops, are undernourished and lack the physical well-being and consequent temperamental buoyancy which are comforting qualities of the well-bred American woman. Unhappy in circumstances, they are predominantly serious in nature, and, if they lack alertness to the social nuance, have yet a compelling appeal which consists in headlong devotion to a duty, a principle, or a person. As their men do not treat them with the scrupulous deference given their American sisters, they do not so delight-

fully abound in their own sense, do not so complex-
edly work out their own natures, and lack variety and
grace. On the other hand, they are more apt to
abound in the sense of something outside of themselves, and carry to their love affairs the same devoted warmth that they put into principle.

THE ORTHODOX JEWESS

The first of the two well-marked classes of women in
the ghetto is that of the ignorant Orthodox Russian
Jewess. She has no language but Yiddish, no learning
but the Talmudic Law, no practical authority but
that of her husband and her rabbi. She is even more
of a *Hausfrau* than the German wife. She can own no
property, and the precepts of the Talmud, as applied

to her conduct, are largely limited to the relations with her husband. Her life is absorbed in observing the religious Law and in taking care of her numerous children. She is drab and plain in appearance, with a thick waist, a wig, and, as far as is possible for a woman, a contempt for ornament. She is, however, with the noticeable assimilative sensitiveness of the Jew, beginning to pick up some of the ways of the American woman. If she is young when she comes to America, she soon lays aside her wig, and sometimes assumes the rakish American hat, prides herself on her bad English, and grows slack in the observance of Jewish holidays and the dietary regulations of the Talmud. Although it is against the Law of this religion to go to the theater, large audiences, mainly drawn from the ignorant workers of the sweatshops and the fishwives and peddlers of the pushcart markets, flock to the Bowery houses. It is this class which forms the large background of the community, the masses from which more cultivated types are developing.

---

Orthodox women tried desperately to fulfill their religious obligations. At the same time, they labored to make the children Americans as quickly as possible. My mother, along with other pious women, began to be suspicious of the ritual slaughtering of the meat. She trusted no butcher. I remember showing my mother a picture of the most famous rabbi in America and she shrugged, "Clean-shaven? You call that a rabbi?"

I had an aunt who was just as pious as my mother, except that she did not have so many children to care for. My aunt Maryam had a daily routine—year in and year out. She got her husband off to work and her daughter off to school, got dressed up and went out looking for a *mitzvah* (a good deed). She looked for a hearse usually, and seeing one she knew there was a funeral somewhere. She found it and went into the house and began to cry and wail over the deceased though not knowing who the dead one was, or even whether it was male or female. But she made a lot of noise about it, and after the funeral she begged for some old clothing of the departed that she delivered to some of the poor in the neighborhood. She spent her entire life adding up these good deeds, and when she got sick, she told us all it was a punishment for a bad thought she had while she was dancing with the handsome Judge Gustave Hartman at the annual ball for the Hebrew Orphan Asylum.

Russian-Jewish women, particularly the younger ones, produced the intellectuals. Mr. Hapgood already knew of their work. These intellectuals had read all the books, and championed the causes of trade unionism, votes for women, and birth control. Some of them were quite effective in their work in settlement houses and on the lecture platform. As early as 1910, Jewish women were parading up and down in front of the state capitol in Albany, demanding an eight-hour day. In those days Margaret Sanger spoke often on the Lower East Side and just as often was arrested. She was trying to convince the immigrant women that they would enjoy better health, live longer lives, rear healthier children, enjoy America more, if they had a baby every two or three years instead of every ten or eleven months. The names of Lillian Wald, Rose Pastor Stokes, Rose Schneiderman, and Lucy Robbins also come to mind. These women were on the lecture platform demanding free textbooks for children, workmen's compensation, and other reforms. Some of their meetings were broken up by the police or by hoodlums hired by political bosses.

Many a literary sketch in the newspapers of the quarter portrays these ignorant, simple, devout, housewifely creatures in comic or pathetic, more often (after the satiric manner of the Jewish writers) in serio-comic vein. The authors, although they are much more educated, yet write of these women, even when they write in comic fashion, with fundamental sympathy. They picture them working devotedly in the shop or at home for their husbands and families; they represent the sorrow and simple jealousy of the wife whose husband's imagination is carried away by the piquant manner and dress of a Jewess who is beginning to ape American ways; they tell of the comic adventures in America of the newly arrived Jewess— how she goes to the theater, perhaps, and enacts the part of Partridge at the play. More fundamentally, they relate how the poor woman is deeply shocked, at her arrival, by the change which a few years have made in the character of her husband, who had come to America before her in order to make a fortune. She finds his beard shaved off, and his manners in regard to religious holidays very slack. She is sometimes so deeply affected that she does not recover. More often she grows to feel the reason and eloquence of the change and becomes partly accustomed to the situation; but all through her life she continues to be dismayed by the precocity, irreligion, and Americanism of her children. Many sketches and many scenes in the ghetto plays present her as a pathetic greenhorn, who, while she is loved by her children, is yet rather patronized and pitied by them.

In *Gott, Mensch und Teufel*, a Yiddish adaptation

of the Faust idea, one of these simple religious souls is dramatically portrayed. The restless Jewish Faust, his soul corrupted by the love of money, puts aside his faithful wife in order to marry another woman who has pleased his eye. He uses as an excuse the fact that his marriage is childless, and as such rendered void in accordance with the precepts of the religious Law. His poor old wife submits almost with reverence to the double authority of husband and Talmud, and with humble demeanor and tears streaming from her eyes begs the privilege of taking care of the children of her successor.

In *The Slaughter* there is a scene which picturesquely portrays the love of the poor Jew and the poor Jewess for their children. The wife is married to a brute, whom she hates, and between the members of the two families there is no relation but that of ugly sordidness. But when it is known that a child is to be born they are all filled with the greatest joy. The husband is ecstatic, and they have a great feast; they drink and sing and dance, and the wife is lyrically happy for the first time since her marriage.

Many little newspaper sketches portray the simple sweatshop Jewess of the ordinary affectionate type, who is exclusively minded so far as her husband's growing interest in the showy American Jewess is concerned. Cahan's novel, *Yekl*, is the ghetto masterpiece in the portrayal of these two types of women— the wronged greenhorn who has just come from Russia, and she who, with a rakish hat and bad English, is becoming an American girl with strange power to alienate the husband's affections.

*Intensely serious*

## THE MODERN TYPE

The other, the educated class of ghetto women, is, of course, in a great minority; and this division includes the women even the most slightly affected by modern ideas as well as those who from an intellectual point of view are highly cultivated. Among the least educated are a large number of women who would be entirely ignorant were it not for the ideas which they have received through the socialist propaganda of the quarter. Like the men who are otherwise ignorant, they are trained to a certain familiarity with economic ideas, read and think a good deal about labor and capital, and take an active part in speaking, in house-to-house distribution of socialistic literature, and in strike agitation. Many of these women, so long as they are unmarried, lead lives thoroughly devoted to "the cause," and afterward become good wives and fruitful mothers, and urge on their husbands and sons to active work in the movement. They have in personal character many virtues called masculine, are simple and straightforward and intensely serious, and do not bank in any way on the fact that they are women! Such a woman would feel insulted if her escort were to pick up her handkerchief or in any way suggest a politeness growing out of the difference in sex. It is from this class of women, from those who are merely tinged, so to speak, with ideas, and who consequently are apt to throw the whole strength of their primitive natures into the narrow intellectual channels that are open to them, that a number of ghetto heroines come who are willing to lay down their lives for an idea, or to live for one. It was only recently that the thinking socialists were stirred by the suicide of a young girl for which several causes were given. Some say it was for love, but what seems a partial cause at least for the tragedy was the girl's devotion to anarchistic ideas. She had worked for some time in the quarter and was filled with enthusiastic Tolstoyan convictions about freedom and nonresistance to evil, and all the other idealistic doctrines for which these anarchists are remarkable. Some of the people of the quarter believe that it was temporary despair of any satisfactory outcome to her work that brought about

*A Russian student*

her death. But since the splits in the Socialist party and the rise among them of many insincere agitators, the enthusiasm for the cause has diminished, particularly among the women, who demand perfect integrity or nothing; though there is still a large class of poor sweatshop women who carry on active propaganda work, make speeches, distribute literature, and go from house to house in a social effort to make converts.

As we ascend in the scale of education in the ghetto, we find women who derive their culture and ideas from a double source—from socialism and from advanced Russian ideals of literature and life. They have lost faith completely in the Orthodox religion, have substituted no other, know Russian better than Yiddish, read Tolstoy, Turgenev, and Chekhov, and often put into practice the most radical theories of the new woman, particularly those which say that woman should be economically independent of man. There are successful female dentists, physicians, writers, and even lawyers by the score in East Broadway who have attained financial independence through industry and intelligence. They are ambitious to a degree and often direct the careers of their husbands or force their lovers to become doctors or lawyers—the great social desiderata in the matchmaking of the ghetto. There is more than one case on record where a girl has compelled her recalcitrant lover to learn law, medicine, or dentistry, or submit to being jilted by her. An actor devoted to the stage is now on the point of leaving it to become a dentist at the command of his ambitious wife. "I always do what she tells me," he said pathetically.

The career of a certain woman now practicing dentistry in the ghetto is one of the most interesting cases, and is also quite typical. She was born of poor Jewish parents in a town near St. Petersburg, and began early to read the socialist propaganda and the Russian literature which contains so much implicit revolutionary doctrine. When she was seventeen years old she wrote a novel in Yiddish, called *Mrs. Goldna, the Usurer,* in which she covertly advocated the anarchistic teachings. The title and the subtheme of the book were directed against the usurer class among the Jews, and were mainly intended to hide from the government her real purpose. The book was afterward published in New York, and had a fairly wide circulation. A year or two later her imagination was irresistibly enthralled by the remarkable wave of new-woman enthusiasm which swept over Russia in the early eighties, and resulted in so many suicides of young girls whom poverty or injustice to the Jew thwarted in their scientific and intellectual ambition. She went alone to St. Petersburg with sixty-five cents in her pocket, in order to obtain a professional education, which, after years of practical starvation, she succeeded in securing. With several degrees she came to America twelve years ago and fought out an independent professional position for herself. She believes that all women should have the means by which they may support themselves, and that marriage under these conditions would be happier than at present. Her husband is a doctor, and her idea is that they are happier than if she were a woman of the old type—"merely a wife and mother," as she put it. She maintains that no emotional interest is lost under the new regime, while many practical advantages are gained. Since she has been in America she has furthered the socialist cause by literary sketches published in the Yiddish newspapers although she has been too busy to take any direct part in the movement.

The description of this type of woman seems rather cold and forbidding in the telling, but such an impression is misleading. There is no commoner reproach made by the women of the ghetto against their American sister than that she is unemotional and "practical." They come to America, like the men, because they cannot stand the political conditions in Russia, which they describe as "fierce," but they never cease loving the land of their birth—and the reason they give is that the ideal still lives in Muscovite civilization, while in America it is trampled out by the cult of the dollar. They think Americans are dry and cold, unpoetic, uninterested in great principles, and essentially frivolous, incapable of devotion

*Working girls return home*

to persons or to movements, reading books only for amusement, and caring nothing for real literature. One day an American dined with four Russian Jews of distinction. Two were nihilists who had been in the big movement in Russia and were merely visiting New York. The other two were a married couple of uncommon education. The nihilists were gentle, cultivated men, with feeling for literature, and deeply admired, because of their connection with the great movement, by the two New Yorkers. The talk turned

*A young Russian*

on Byron, for whom the Russians had a warm enthusiasm. The Americans made rather light of Byron and incurred thereby the great scorn of the Russians, who felt deeply the "tendency" character of the poet without being able to understand his esthetic and imaginative limitations. After the nihilists had left, the misguided American used the words "interesting" and "amusing" in connection with them; whereupon the Russian lady was almost indignant, and dilated on the frivolity of a race that could not take serious people seriously, but wanted always to be entertained; that cared only for what was "pretty" and "charming" and "sensible" and "practical," and cared nothing for poetry and beauty and essential humanity.

The woman referred to, as well as many others of the most educated class in the quarter, some of them the wives of socialists, doctors, lawyers or literary men, are strongly interesting because of their warm temperaments, and genuine, if limited, ideas about art; but most of them are lacking in grace, and sense of humor and of proportion. They are stiff and unyielding, have little free play of imagination, little alertness of ideas, and their sense of literature is limited largely to realism. Japanese art, for instance, as any art which depends on the exquisiteness of its form, is lost on these stern realists. They no more understand the latest subtle literary consciousness than they do the interest and eloquence of a creature who makes of herself a perfect social product such as the clever French woman of history.

But the charm of sincere feeling they have; and, in

an intellectual race, that feeling shapes itself into definite criticism of society. Emotionally strong and attached by Russian tradition to a rebellious doctrine, they are deeply unconventional in theory and sometimes in practice, although the national morality of the Jewish race very definitely limits the extent to which they realize some of their ideas. The passionate feeling at the bottom of most of their "tendency" beliefs is that woman should stand on the same social basis as man and should be weighed on the same scales. This ruling creed is held by all classes of the educated women of the ghetto, from the poor sweatshop worker who has recently felt the influence of socialism, to the thoroughly trained new woman with her developed literary taste; and all its variations find expression in the literature of the quarter.

## PLACE OF WOMAN IN GHETTO LITERATURE

Ibsen's *Doll House* has been translated and produced at a Yiddish theater; and an original play called *Minna* registers a protest by the Jewish woman against that law of marriage which binds her to an inferior man. Married to an ignorant laborer, Minna falls in love (for his advanced ideas) with the boarder (every poor family, to pay the rent, must saddle itself with a boarder, often at the expense of domestic happiness) and finally kills herself when the laws of society press her too hard.

Incidentally, the male boarder occupied a unique and important position in the immigrant culture. Once he moved in, he quickly became a familiar. He even had authority to spank misbehaving children. Wherever the family went, the boarder went, too. He knew the ins and outs, the joys and sorrows, and could often step between a quarreling husband and wife. Families with a marriageable daughter picked a boarder with the idea of marrying her off. But once a boarder committed himself he had to follow through. If he took the girl out once or twice and lost interest, he moved out to save face in the girl's family and save himself from an involvement that could lead only to the wedding canopy.

Another drama called *East Broadway* presents the case of a Russian Jewess devoted to Russia, to idealism and nihilism, and to a man who shared her faith until they came to New York, when he became a businessman pure and simple, and lost his ideals and his love for her. In a popular play called *The Beggar of Odessa*, lines openly advocating the freest love between the sexes accompany other extreme anarchistic views put into the loosest and most popular form. *Broken Chains* is a drama which criticizes the relative freedom of action given to the man in matters of love. The heroine reads Ibsen at night while her husband amuses himself in the quarter. A young bookkeeper is there who serves to make concrete her growing theories. But her sense of duty to her child restrains her from the final step, and she dies in despair. Suicides in sketches and plays abound, and as often as not result simply from intellectual despondency. *A Vain Sacrifice* is the fierce outcry of a woman against the poverty which makes her marry a man she loathes for the sake of her father. In the newspaper sketches there are many pictures of sordid homes and conditions from the midst of which fierce protests by wives and mothers are implicitly given.

An appealing characteristic of the new woman of the ghetto is the consideration which she manifests toward the Orthodox greenhorn who may be her aunt, her mother, her mother-in-law, or her grandmother. The sense of infinite form prescribed by the Talmud is dead to her, but extraordinary love for the family bond is not, and, moved by that, she observes the complicated formulas on all the holidays in order to please the dear old greenhorn who lives with her— eats unleavened bread, weeps on Atonement Day in the synagogue, and goes through the whole long list. Her conduct in this respect is in striking contrast to the offhand treatment of parents by their American daughters, and to that of the Orthodox Jewish woman in relation to the theater. The Law forbids the theater, but even the slightly disillusioned ladies of the quarter will go on the Sabbath; and it is said that they sometimes hypocritically relieve their consciences by hissing the actor who, even in his role, dares to smoke on that day. This is on a par with the hypocrisy which leads many Orthodox Jewish families to have a Gentile as their servant, so that they can drink the tea and warm themselves by the fire, made by him, without technically violating the Law.

Love in the ghetto is, no doubt, very much the same as it is elsewhere; and this in spite of the fact that among the Orthodox marriage is arranged by the parents, a custom which is condemned in *The Slaughter*, for instance, where the terrible results of a loveless union are portrayed. The system of matrimonial agents in the quarter does not seem to have any important bearing on the question of love. In this respect the free thinking of the people grows apace, and love marriages in the quarter are on the increase. In matters of taste and inclination between the sexes, however, there are some qualities quite startling to the American. The most popular actor with the girls of the ghetto is a very fat, heavy, pompous hero who would provoke only a smile from the trim American girl, and the more popular actresses are also very stout ladies. From an American point of view, the prettiest actresses of the ghetto are admired by the minority of Jews who have been taken by the rakish hat, the slim form, and the indefinite charm to which the ghetto is being educated. It is alleged that at an uptown theater, where a large proportion of the audience is Jewish, the leading lady must always be of very generous build; and this in spite of the fact that the well-to-do Jews uptown have been in America a long time and have had ample opportunity to become smitten with the charms of the slender American girl.

---

The wedding was an event remembered for years to come. People waited in hushed expectancy for the signal, "They are leading the bride." Everybody turned to the end of the hall where the bride, attended by maids and relatives and perhaps a dozen hangers-on, began her march to the wedding canopy.

Half an hour later someone announced, "The groom is

coming." He was surrounded by at least two uncles and his father in addition to his brothers, friends, fellow workers, and the social director from the settlement house. It was considered a formal insult not to invite all the neighbors to a wedding. All night long jovial *mazeltovs* rang through the celebration.

The Orthodox Jewish wedding was a theological manifestation. One of the questions all Jews have to answer is, "In how many days did the Holy One, blessed be He, create the universe?"

The student answers, "In six days did He create the universe."

"What has He, the Blessed One, done since?"

And the answer, the only answer: "Since then He has been arranging marriages."

Romance and marriage, however, were often two different things. The Jewish maidens fell in love with the leading ghetto actors. Any actor who was fat and heavy was always popular with the girls. Young girls and old girls had a dreamy look when they saw a picture of Boris Thomashevsky wearing tights. Boris was a big man, lots of weight.

The first words a Jewish child heard were, *"Ess, ess mein Kindt* [Eat, eat, my child]." A fifteen-year-old boy already weighing one hundred and forty-five pounds was an object of concern to his mother if he dawdled over his supper. "Look at him, nothing but skin and bones," said Mama, near tears. Young ladies practiced sitting postures that would accentuate flesh and heft. And when you went off on a week's vacation, the first question everybody asked you when you returned was "How much did you gain?"

I was a fat kid myself and I remember my mother saying, "In America the fat man is the boss and the skinny man is the bookkeeper."

Weight and food were intimately related to the Jewish idea of survival. But I suspect now that this concern for eating and heft was in some way related to the fear of tuberculosis. This terrible disease took a frightful toll of the East Side sweatshop workers. One of the early symptoms was lack of appetite, loss of weight. The mother watched the weight of all the family, the factory workers among us, the children, the boarders. She wanted everybody fat, which to her meant—no tuberculosis.

I'd like to expand a little on this aspect of ghetto life that Mr. Hapgood could not yet see in 1902. The East Side doctor had to be also a social worker and a philosopher. He diagnosed the tuberculosis of the father of the house and he saw the wife and four children, all young ones, another child on the way—and he knew what those weekly wages meant to that family. Could he tell this man to stop working or take a vacation? There was no union welfare fund or disability social security yet; so the doctor prescribed cough medicine and told the man: "Rest, lie down, rest every chance you get." One *verein* doctor added to every prescription the words, "Join the union." Eventually the unions provided for hospitalization and treatment, and later on many afflicted workingmen went out to the National Jewish Hospital at Denver, Colorado.

But to return. Most marriages in the early days were contracted through a matchmaker. The system gradually diminished and disappeared entirely in the second generation.

The *shadkhan* (matchmaker) entered into preliminary negotiations with the parents. After these discussions, the parents of the girl told her about them and a formal meeting was arranged. The East Side joke was: at the age of eighteen, she asks, "What does he look like?"; at twenty-five, she asks, "What does he do for a living?"; and at thirty, "Where is he?" The *shadkhan's* biggest headache was the amateur competition. Everybody was a part-time *shadkhan.*

Marrying off a daughter was the greatest of anxieties.

Anxiety increased with each additional daughter. Daughters had to be married off in sequence, the oldest first. No problem was a match for the problems of a father whose youngest daughter was the prettiest. I've known cases where the pretty younger sister was sent out of the house to visit relatives when a young man called on the oldest daughter.

The first thing a young man would ask of a *shadkhan* was "Is she pretty?" and the second question he asked was "How about a dowry?" Lucky was the girl who had several brothers out earning money. Everybody chipped in to provide her with a dowry.

# FOUR POETS

In East Canal Street, in the heart of the East Side, are many of the little Russian Jewish cafés, already mentioned, where excellent coffee and tea are sold, where everything is clean and good, and where the conversation is often of the best. The talk is good, for there assemble, in the late afternoon and evening, the chosen crowd of intellectuals. The best that is Russian today is intensely serious. What is distinctively Jewish has always been serious. The man hunted from his country is apt to have a serious tone in thought and feeling.

It is this combination—Russian, Jewish, and exile —that is represented at these little Canal Street cafés. The somber and earnest qualities of the race, emphasized by the special conditions, receive here expression in the mouths of actors, socialists, musicians, journalists, and poets. Here they get together and talk by the hour, over their coffee and cake, about politics and society, poetry and ethics, literature and life. The cafékeepers themselves are thoughtful and often join in the discussion—a discussion never light but sometimes lighted up by bitter wit and gloomy irony.

There are many poets among them, four of whom stand out as men of great talent. One of the four, Morris Rosenfeld, is already well known to the English-speaking world through a translation of some of his poems. Two of the other three are equally well known, but only to the Jewish people. One is famous throughout Jewish Russia.

---

The boys who dodged between the pushcarts in the Jewish ghetto wrote many of America's popular songs: "Carolina Moon," "Swanee," "Alabam'," and hundreds of others. One of these, Wolfie Gilbert, my good friend who wrote, "Waiting for the Robert E. Lee," wrote me forty years later to ask, "Harry, now that you are down South, please let me know what is a levee?"

The first of these East Side boys to put the spirit of America to popular music was Irving Berlin. Son of a synagogue cantor, Isador Balin was a saloon song plugger whose first tune earned him thirty-seven cents. His earliest songs concerned the immigrants: "Marie from Sunny Italy," "Oh, How That German Could Love," and "Yiddishe Eyes."

"Alexander's Ragtime Band" put him on the road to fame in 1910. Americans marched off to World Wars I and II singing, "Oh, How I Hate To Get Up in the Morning," and "This is the Army, Mr. Jones." Berlin's "God Bless America" is virtually a second national anthem.

---

A WEDDING BARD

The oldest of the four poets is Eliakim Zunser. It is he that is known to millions of people in Russia and

*Eliakim Zunser*

to the whole New York ghetto. He is the poet of the common people, the beloved of all, the poet of the housewife, of the Jew who is so ignorant that he does not even know his own family name. To still more ignorant people, if such are possible, he is known by what, after all, is his distinctive title, Eliakim the *badchen*, or the wedding bard. He writes in Yiddish, the universal language of the Jew, dubbed "jargon" by the Hebrew aristocrat.

Zunser is now a printer in Rutger's Square, and has largely given up his duties as *badchen*, but at one time he was so famous in that capacity that he went to a wedding once or twice every day, and made in that way a large income. His part at the ceremony was to address the bride and bridegroom in verse so solemn that it would bring tears to their eyes, and then entertain the guests with burlesque lines. He composed the music as well as the verses and did both extempore. When he left his home to attend the wedding, there was no idea in his head as to what he would say. He left that to the result of a hurried talk before the ceremony with the wedding guests and the relatives of the couple.

Zunser's wedding verses died as soon as they were born, but there are sixty-five collections of his poems, hundreds of which are sung every day to young and old throughout Russia. Many others have never been published, for Zunser is a poet who composes as he breathes, whose every feeling and idea quivers into poetic expression, and who preserves only an accidental part of what he does.

He is a man of about seventy years of age, with kind little eyes, a gray beard, and spare, short figure. As he sits in his printing office in the far East Side he wears a small black cap on his head. Adjoining the office is another room, in which he lives with his wife and several children. The stove, the dining table, the beds, are all in the same room, which is bare and chill. But the poet is hospitable, and to the guests he offered cake and a bottle of sarsaparilla. Far more delightful, however, the old man read some of his poems aloud. As he read in a chanting tone he swayed gently backward and forward unconscious of his visitors, absorbed in the rhythm and feeling of the song. There was great sweetness and tenderness in his eyes, facility and spontaneity in the meter, and simple pathos and philosophy in the meaning of what he said. He was apparently not conscious of the possession of unusual power. Famous as he is, there was no sense of it in his bearing. He is absolutely of the people, childlike and simple. So far removed is he from the pride of his distinction that he has largely given up poetry now.

"I don't write much any more," he said in his careless Yiddish. "I have not much time."

His poetry seemed to him only a detail of his life. Along with the simplicity of old age he has the maturity and aloofness of it. The feeling for his position as an individual, if he ever had it, has gone, and left the mind and heart interested only in God, race, and impersonal beauty.

So as he chanted his poems he seemed to gather up into himself the dignity and pathos of his serious and suffering race, but as one who had gone beyond suffering and lived only with the eternities. His wife and children bent over him as he recited, and their bodies kept time with his rhythm. One of the two visitors was a Jew, whose childhood had been spent in Russia, and when Zunser read a dirge which he had composed in Russia twenty-five years ago at the death by cholera of his first wife and children—a dirge which is now chanted daily in thousands of Jewish homes in Russia—the visitor joined in, although he had not heard it for many years. Tears came to his eyes as memories of his childhood were brought up by Zunser's famous lines; his body swayed to and fro in sympathy with that of Zunser and those of the poet's second wife and her children; and to the Anglo-Saxon present this little group of Jewish exiles moved by rhythm, pathos, and the memory of a faraway land conveyed a strange emotion.

Zunser's dirge is in a vein of reflective melancholy.

"The Mail Wagon" is its title. The mail wagon brings joy and sorrow, hope and despair, and it was this awful mechanism that brought Zunser's grief home to him. "But earth, too, is a machine, a machine that crushes the bones of the philosopher into dust, digests them, that crushes and digest all things. From it all comes. Into it all goes. Why may I not therefore be chewing at this moment the marrow of my children?"

Another song the old man read aloud was composed in his early childhood, and is representative in subject and mood of much of his later work. "The Song of the Bird," it is called, and it typifies the Jewish race. The bird's wing is broken, and the bird reflects in tender melancholy over his misfortunes. "Take me away from Rumania" has the same melancholy, but also a humorous pathos in the title, for the poet meant he would like to be taken away from Russia, but was afraid to say so for political reasons. But the sadness of Zunser's poetry is lightened by its spontaneity and by the felicity of verse and music, and the naive idea in each poem is never too solemnly insisted upon for popular poetry.

The dirge, which touched upon an episode of his life, led the poet to tell in his simple way the other events of a life history at once typical and peculiar.

He was born in Vilnyus, the capital of ancient Lithuania, and became an apprentice to a weaver of gold lace at the age of six. His general education was consequently slight, though he picked up a little of the Talmud and sang Isaiah and Jeremiah while at work. At the end of six years, when he was supposed to know his trade, his master was to give him twenty rubles as total wage. But the master refused to pay, and young Zunser took to the road with no money. He went to Bysk in the Ostsee province, and there worked at his trade during the day, and at night studied the Talmud under the local rabbi. He also began to read books in pure Hebrew for the love of the noble poetry in that tongue. Before long he received word from home that his little brother had died. He went back and helped his mother cry, as he expressed it. Away he went again from home to a place called Bobroysk, where he obtained a position to teach Hebrew to the family of an innkeeper, who promised to pay him twenty-five rubles at the end of six months. When the time came his employer said he would pay at the end of the year. Ingenuous Zunser agreed, but the innkeeper, just before the end of the year, went to a government official and reported that there was a boy at his house who was fit to be a soldier. Young Zunser was pressed into the service. He was then thirteen. It was in the barracks that he composed his first three songs. In these songs he poured out his heart, told all his woe, but did not print them, "for," he said, "it was my own case."

On being released from the service, Zunser went to Vilnyus and continued his trade as a gold-lace maker. He also wrote many poems and songs. They were not printed at first, but circulated in written copies. Zunser is said to be the first man to write songs in Yiddish, and soon he became famous. "It was 'the lacemaker boy' everywhere," as the poet expressed it. Now that he could make money by his songs he gave up his trade and devoted himself to art. In 1861 he returned to his native town a great man. There he first saw his work in print. Then came a period when he wrote a great deal and performed every day his function as wedding bard. For ten years things prospered with him, but in 1871 his wife and four children died of cholera. Zunser composed the famous dirge, left Vilnyus, which appeared to him unlucky, and went to Minsk. Here he continued to get a living with his pen, and married again. Ten years ago he came to New York with his family and kept up his occupation as wedding bard for some time.

The character of Zunser's poetry is what might be expected from his popularity, slight education, and humble position in the Jewish world. His melancholy is common to all Jewish poets. There is a constant reference to his race, too, a love for it, and a sort of humble pride. More than any of the four poets whom we are to mention, with the possible exception of Morris Rosenfeld, Zunser has a fresh lyric quality which has gone far to endear him to the people. Yet in spite of his sweet birdlike speed of expression, Zunser's is a poetry of ideas although the ideas are simple, fragmentary, and fanciful, and are seldom sustained beyond what is admissible to the lyric touch. The pale cast of thought, less marked in Zunser's work than in that of the other three poets, is also a common characteristic of Jewish poetry. Melancholy, patriotic, and thoughtful, what is lacking in Zunser is what all modern Jewish poetry lacks and what forms a sweet part of Anglo-Saxon literature—

the distinctively sensuous element. A Keats is a Hebrew impossibility. The poetry of simple presentation, of the qualities of mere physical nature, is strikingly absent of the imaginative work of this serious and moral people. The intellectual element is always noticeable, even in simple Zunser, the poet of the people.

## A CHAMPION OF RACE

A striking contrast to the popular wedding bard is Menahem Dolitzki, called the Hebrew poet because he has the distinction of writing in the old Hebrew language.

His learning is limited to the old literature of his race. He is not a generally well-educated man, not

*Menahem Dolitzki*

knowing or caring anything about modern life or ideas. The poet of the holy tongue, he is what the Jews call *maskil* (man of wisdom). The aloof dignity of his position fills him with a mild contempt for the "jargon," the Yiddish of Rosenfeld and Zunser, and makes him distrustful of what the fourth poet, Wald, represents—the modern socialistic spirit.

Singularly enough, he is called by the socialists of the ghetto the poet of the dilettanti. An Anglo-Saxon American employs the term to mean those persons superficially interested in much, deeply interested in nothing; but these socialistic spirits stigmatize as "dilettante" whatever is not immersed in the spirit of the modern world. The man of form, the lover of the old, the cool man with scholastic tinge have no place in the sympathetic imagination of the ghetto intellectuals. They leave him to the learned among old fogies. And it is true that Dolitzki's appeal is a limited one, both as a man and as a poet. He is a handsome man of about forty-five years, with a fine profile, an unenthusiastic manner, a native reserve very evident in his way of reading his poetry. He has nothing of the buoyant spontaneity, the personal feeling of Zunser. The poet of the people was a part of his verse as he read. He threw himself into it, identified himself with his musical and fanciful creation. But Dolitzki, who has been recently a traveling agent for a Yiddish newspaper on the East Side, and has a little home suggesting greater cleanliness and comfort than that of Zunser, held his manuscript at arm's length and read his verses with no apparent sign of emotion. About his poetry and life he talked with comparative reserve, in the former evidently caring most for the form and the language, and in the latter for the ideas which determined his intellectual life rather than for picturesque details and events.

Dolitzki's life and work are identified with the revival of Hebrew literature of fifty years ago, and, more narrowly, of twenty years ago. He is one of the great poets of that revival, and wherever it is felt in the Jewish world, there Dolitzki is known and admired. He was born in Bialystok, but spent his early manhood in Moscow, whence he was expelled. That event partly determined the character of his first writings—patriotic poems of culture, reasoned outcries against the religious prejudice of the Orthodox Jews, the Jews who take their stand on the Talmud, led by the hair-splitting rabbi, upholders of the narrow Jewish theology. Just as the revival of learning in Europe brought doubt of orthodoxy along with it, so the revival of the pure Hebrew literature brought doubt of the religion of the established rabbi, founded on a minute interpretation of the Talmud. The Hebrew scholars who went back to the sources of Jewish literature for their inspiration were worse than infidels to the Orthodox. And Dolitzki was the poet of these infidels.

When, however, the Jews were expelled from Moscow, Dolitzki's interest broadened to love of his race. It is not so much interest in human nature that these noble and austere poems manifest, as an epic love for the race as a whole, a lofty and abstract emotion. The intellectual and moral element characteristic of Jewish poetry is particularly marked in Dolitzki's work. His first poems, those of culture inspired by hatred of Talmudic prejudice, and his later ones, filled with the abstract love of his race, are poems of idealism expressed largely in complicated symbolical language, lacking, as compared with Zunser's poetry, spontaneity, wholly wanting in sensuous imagery, but written in musical and finished verse.

A poem illustrating Dolitzki's first period tells how a cherub bore the poet, symbolizing the Jewish people, aloft, where he could see pure and beautiful things, but soon the earth appeared, in the shape of a round loaf of bread symbolizing need and poverty and prejudice; and to this the aspiring Jew must return and from this he could not escape. One of the poems in which Dolitzki's love of his race is expressed describes a man and a maiden who, driven by love of one another and fear of oppression, are sitting upon a lofty rock. Below them on the plain they see their families murdered by the invaders. Then they voluntarily die, declaring that they will yet live forever in the race.

Dolitzki's remote idealism represents a nobler kind of thing than what is generally associated with the East Side. A dignified and epic poet, he is filled with moral rather than enthusiastic love of the old language and the old race.

## A SINGER OF LABOR

Morris Rosenfeld, poet and former tailor, strikes in his personality and writings the weary minor. Full of

*Morris Rosenfeld*

tears are the man and his song. Zunser, Dolitzki, and
Wald, although in their verse runs the eternal melancholy of poetry and of the Jews, have yet physical
buoyancy and a robust spirit. But Rosenfeld, small,
dark, and fragile in body, with fine eyes and drooping
eyelashes, and a plaintive, childlike voice, is weary
and sick—a simple poet, a sensitive child, a bearer of
burdens, an East Side tailor. Zunser and Dolitzki
have shown themselves able to cope with their hard
conditions, but the sad little Rosenfeld, unpractical
and incapable in all but his songs, has had the hard-
est time of all. His life has been typical of that of
many a delicate poet—a life of privation, of struggle
borne by weak shoulders, and a spirit and temperament not fitted to meet the world.

Much younger than Zunser or Dolitzki, Morris Rosenfeld was born thirty-eight years ago in a small village in the province of Subalk, in Russian Poland, at the end of the last Polish revolution. The very night he was born the world began to oppress him, for insurgents threw rocks through the window. His grandfather was rich, but his father lost the money in business, and Morris received very little education —only the Talmud and a little German, which he got at school in Warsaw. He married when he was sixteen "because my father told me to," as the poet expressed it. He ran away from Poland to avoid being pressed into the army. "I would like to serve my country," he said, "if there had been any freedom for the Jew." Then he went to Holland and learned the trade of diamond cutting, then to London, where he took up tailoring.

Hearing that the tailors had won a strike in America, he came to New York, thinking he would need to work here only ten hours a day. "But what I heard," he said, "was a lie. I found the sweatshops in New York just as bad as they were in London."

In those places he worked for many years, worked away his health and strength, but at the same time composed many a sweetly sad song. "I worked in the sweatshop in the daytime," he said to me, "and at night I worked at my poems. I could not help writing them. My heart was full of bitterness. If my poems are sad and plaintive, it is because I expressed my own feelings, and because my surroundings were sad."

Next to Zunser, Rosenfeld is the most popular of

the four Jewish poets. Zunser is most popular in Russia, Rosenfeld in this country. Both write in the universal Yiddish, both are simple and spontaneous, musical and untutored. But, unlike Zunser, Rosenfeld is a thorough representative, one might say victim, of the modern spirit. Zunser sings to an older and more buoyant Jewish world, to the Russian Hebrew village and the country at large. Rosenfeld in weary accents sings to the maimed spirit of the Jewish slums. It is a fresh, naive note, the pathetic cry of the bright spirit crushed in the poisonous air of the ghetto. The first song that Rosenfeld printed in English is this:

*I lift mine eyes against the sky,*
*The clouds are weeping, so am I.*
*I lift mine eyes again on high,*
*The sun is smiling, so am I.*
*Why do I smile? Why do I weep?*
*I do not know; it lies too deep.*

*I hear the winds of autumn sigh,*
*They break my heart, they make me cry.*
*I hear the birds of lovely spring,*
*My hopes revive, I help them sing.*
*Why do I sing? Why do I cry?*
*It lies so deep, I know not why.*

---

In a biography of Sir Jacob Epstein by Richard Buckle (The World Publishing Company, 1963), the author refers to the sculptor's first published work, which appeared "in a naive book by Hutchins Hapgood," meaning Mr. Buckle thinks this a "sentimental" book. But it was Mr. Hapgood who first recognized the talent and the importance of nineteen-year-old Jacob Epstein, and Mr. Hapgood was also the first non-Jewish critic to recognize the talent and the importance of the poet Morris Rosenfeld. "Sentimental" perhaps; "naive" no.

Since Hapgood's days, Morris Rosenfeld has been one of the most widely translated Yiddish poets not only in English but into other languages. The most recent translation of his work in English was issued in 1964 by the *Yiddisher Kultur Farband* of New York, edited by Itche Goldberg and Max Rosenfeld.

Rosenfeld produced a vast amount of poetry. His early critics contended he was not a Jewish poet but a workingman's poet. Rosenfeld wrote in the laborer's idiom in a diction a workingman could understand.

These critics were friendly critics—Gentiles in the labor movement, who wanted Rosenfeld for their own. "He is a class poet," they said, "a worker's poet." These friendly critics cite as an example Rosenfeld's "All for Naught":

*Smash your pen, wretched poet!*
*Who needs your song, your lyric art,*
*In this discordant, frantic land*
*Which clamors like a noisy mart,*
*Where frenzied people rush about,*
*Where every sound's a hue and cry,*
*Where every man lives by his wits*
*And barely has the time to die.*

---

*Abraham Wald*

### A DREAMER OF BROTHERHOOD

Abraham Wald, whose nom de plume is Lessin, is only twenty-eight years old, the youngest and least known of the four poets, yet in some respects the most interesting. He is the only one who is on a level with the intellectual alertness of the day. His education is broad and in some directions thorough. He is the only one of the four poets whom we are discussing who knows Russian, which language he often writes. He is an imaginative critic, a violent socialist, and an excitable lover of nature.

One of his friends called the poet on one occasion an intellectual debauchee. It was in a Canal Street café, where Wald was talking in an excited tone to several other intellectuals. He is a short, stocky man, with a suggestion of physical power. His eyes are brilliant, and there seems to be going on in him a sort of intellectual consumption. He is restlessly intense in manner, speaks in images, and is always passionately convinced of the truth of what he sees so clearly but seldom expresses in cold logic. His fevered idealism meets you in his frank, quick gaze and impulsive, rapid speech.

Lacking in repose, balance, and sobriety of thought, Wald is well described by his friend's phrase. Equally well he may be called the Jewish bohemian. He is not dissipated in the ordinary sense. Coffee and tea are the drinks he finds in his little cafés. But in these places he practically lives, disputing, arguing, expounding, with whomsoever he may find. He has no fixed home, but sleeps wherever inevitable weariness finds him. He prefers to sleep not at all. Like all his talented tribe, he is poor and makes an occasional dollar by writing a poem or an article for an East Side newspaper. When he has collected three or four dollars he quits the newspaper office and seeks again his beloved café, violently to impart his quick-coming thoughts and impulses. Only after his money is gone—and it lasts him many days—does he return to his work on the paper, the editor of which must be an uncommonly good-natured fellow.

Impelled by political reasons, Wald left Russia three years ago, but before that time, which was in his twenty-fifth year, he had passed through eight mental and moral crises. Perhaps the number was a poetical exaggeration, for when I asked the poet to enumerate he gave only five. As a boy he revolted from the hair-splitting Talmudic Orthodoxy, and was cursed in consequence; then he lost his Jewish faith altogether; then his whole Kulturanschauung changed, on account of the influence of Russian literature. He became an atheist and then a socialist and perhaps a pantheist—at least he has written poems in which breathes the personified spirit of nature. Without the peace of nature, however, is the man and his work. He dislikes America because it lacks the ebullient activity of moral, imaginative life. Wald likes Russia better than America because Russia, to use the poet's words, is idealism and hope, and America is realization.

"Before I came to America," he said, "I thought it would not be as interesting as Russia, and when I got here I saw that I was right. America seemed all worked out to me, as if mighty things had already been done, but it seemed lifeless at the core. Russia, on the other hand, with no external form of national prosperity, is all activity at heart, restless longing. Russia is nothing to see, but alive and bubbling at the core. The American wants a legal wife, something there and sure, but the Russian wants a wife behind a mountain, through which he cannot penetrate, but can only dream and strive for her."

These four poets have what is distinctive of Jewish poetry—the pulse of desire and hope, in which there is strain and reproach, constant effort. The Russian Jew's lack of appreciation of completed beauty or of merely sensuous nature is strikingly illustrated by the fact that there has never been a great expression of plastic art in his history. Painting, sculpture, and architecture are nothing to the Jew in comparison with the literature and music of ideas. In nearly all the Jews of talent I have met, there is the same intellectual consumption, the excitement of beauty, but no enjoyment of pure beauty of form. The race is still too unhappy, too unsatisfied, has too much to gain, to express a complacent sense of the beauty of what is.

Wald's is the poetry of socialism and of nature, and one form is as turbulent as the other. He writes, for instance, of the prisoner in Siberia, his verses filled with passionate rebellion. Then he tells how he dreamed beside the gleaming river, and of the fancies that passed through his brain—not merely pretty fancies, but passionately moral images in which rebellion, longing, wonder, are by turns expressed; never peaceful enjoyment of nature, never simply the humble eye that sees and questions not, but always the moral storm and stress.

Wald and Rosenfeld represent at once things similar and unlike. Both are associated with the modern spirit of socialism, both are identified with the heart of big cities, both are very civilized, yet in temperament and quality no two poets could be more widely separated. Rosenfeld is the finer spirit, the more narrow, too. He is eminently the ghetto Jew. But Wald, as one sees him talking in the café, his whole body alive with emotion, with his youthful, open face, his constant energy, and the modernity and freshness of his ideas, seems the Russian rather than the Jew, and suggests the vivid spirit of Tolstoy.

In comparison with Wald and Rosenfeld the older men, Dolitzki and Zunser, seem remote. Dolitzki has the remoteness of culture and Zunser that of old age and relative peace of spirit. But compared among themselves the poets of the four are Zunser and Rosenfeld, the spontaneous lyric singers. Wald, however, is making his way rapidly into the sympathetic intelligence of the socialists—a growing class—but has not as yet the same wide appeal as the two poets who sing only in the tongue of the people.

# five

# THE STAGE

## THEATERS, ACTORS, AND AUDIENCE

In the three Yiddish theaters on the Bowery is expressed the world of the ghetto—that New York city of Russian Jews, large, complex, with a full life and civilization. In the midst of the frivolous Bowery, devoted to tinsel variety shows, "dive" music-halls, fake museums, trivial amusement booths of all sorts, cheap lodging houses, ten-cent shops and Irish-American tough saloons, the theaters of the chosen people alone present the serious as well as the trivial interests of an entire community. Into these three buildings crowd the Jews of all the ghetto classes—the sweatshop woman with her baby, the day laborer, the small Hester Street shopkeeper, the Russian-Jewish anarchist and socialist, the ghetto rabbi and scholar, the poet, the journalist. The poor and ignorant are in the great majority, but the learned, the intellectual, and the progressive are also represented, and here, as elsewhere, exert a more than numerically proportionate influence on the character of the theatrical productions, which, nevertheless, remain essentially popular. The socialists and the literati create the demand that forces into the mass of vaudeville, light opera and historical and melodramatic plays a more serious art element, a simple transcript from life or the theatric presentation of a ghetto problem. But this more serious element is so saturated with the simple manners, humor, and pathos of the life of the poor Jew that it is seldom above the heartfelt understanding of the crowd.

The audiences vary in character from night to night rather more than in an uptown theater. On the evenings of the first four week days the theater is let to a guild or club, many hundred of which exist among the working people of the East Side. Many are labor organizations representing the different trades, many are purely social, and others are in the nature of secret societies. Some of these clubs are formed on the basis of a common home in Russia. The people, for instance, who came from Vilnyus, a city in the old country, have organized a Vilnyus Club in the ghetto. Then, too, the anarchists have a society; there are many socialistic orders; the newspapers of the ghetto have their constituency, which sometimes hires the theater. Two or three hundred dollars is paid to the theater by the guild, which then sells the tickets among the faithful for a good price. Every member of the society is forced to buy, whether he wants to see the play or not, and the money made over and above the expenses of hiring the theater is for the benefit of the guild. These performances are therefore called benefits. The widespread existence of such a custom is a striking indication of the growing sense of corporate interests among the laboring classes of the Jewish East Side. It is an expression of the socialistic spirit which is marked everywhere in the ghetto.

On Friday, Saturday, and Sunday nights the theater is not let, for these are the Jewish holidays, and the house is always completely sold out, although prices range from twenty-five cents to a dollar. Friday night is, properly speaking, the gala occasion of the week. That is the legitimate Jewish holiday, the night before the Sabbath. Orthodox Jews, as well as others, may then amuse themselves. Saturday, although the day of worship, is also of holiday character in the ghetto. This is due to the Christian influ-

*The theater*

ences, to which the Jews are more and more sensitive. Through economic necessity Jewish workingmen are compelled to work on Saturday, and, like other workingmen, look upon Saturday night as a holiday, in spite of the frown of the Orthodox. Into Sunday, too, they extend their freedom, and so in the ghetto there are three popularly recognized nights on which to go with all the world to the theater.

On those nights the theater presents a peculiarly picturesque sight. Poor workingmen and women with their babies of all ages fill the theater. Great enthusiasm is manifested, sincere laughter and tears accompany the sincere acting on the stage. Peddlers of soda water, candy, of fantastic gewgaws of many kinds, mix freely with the audience between the acts. Conversation during the play is received with strenuous hisses, but the falling of the curtain is the signal for groups of friends to get together and gossip about the play or the affairs of the week. Introductions are not necessary, and the Yiddish community can then be seen and approached with great freedom. On the stage curtain are advertisements of the wares of Hester Street or portraits of the star actors. On the programs and circulars distributed in the audience are sometimes amusing announcements of coming attractions or lyric praise of the stars. Poetry is not infrequent; an example literally translated is:

*Labor, ye stars, as ye will,*
*Ye cannot equal the artist.*
*In the garden of art ye shall not flourish,*
*Ye can never achieve his fame.*

*Can you play* Hamlet *like him?*
*The* Wild King? *Or the* Huguenots?
*Are you gifted with feeling*
*So much as to imitate him like a shadow?*
*Your fame rests on the pen;*
*On the showcards your flight is high,*
*But on the stage every one can see*
*How your greatness turns to ashes,*
*Tomashevsky! Artist great!*
*No praise is good enough for you;*
*Everyone remains your ardent friend.*
*Of all the stars you remain the king.*
*You seek no tricks, no false quibbles.*
*One sees Truth itself playing.*
*Your appearance is godly to us,*
*Every movement is full of grace,*
*Pleasing is your every gesture;*
*Sugar sweet your every turn.*
*You remain the king of the stage;*
*Everything falls to your feet.*

On the playboards outside the theater, containing usually the portrait of a star, are also lyric and enthusiastic announcements. Thus, on the return of the great Adler, who had been ill, it was announced on the boards that "the splendid eagle has spread his wings again."

The Yiddish actors, as may be inferred from the verses quoted, take themselves with peculiar seriousness, justified by the enthusiasm, almost worship, with which they are regarded by the people. Many a poor Jew, man or girl, who makes no more than ten dollars a week in the sweatshop, will spend five dollars of it on the theater, which is practically the only amusement of the ghetto Jew. He has not the loafing and sporting instincts of the poor Christian, and spends his money for the theater rather than for drink. It is not only to see the play that the poor Jew goes to the theater. It is to see his friends and the actors. With these latter he, and more frequently she, trys in every way to make acquaintance, but commonly is compelled to adore at a distance. They love the songs that are heard on the stage, and for these the demand is so great that a certain bookshop on the East Side makes a specialty of publishing them.

The actor responds to this popular enthusiasm with sovereign contempt. He struts about in the cafés on Canal and Grand streets, conscious of his greatness. He refers to the crowd as Moses, with superior condescension or humorous vituperation. Like thieves, the actors have a jargon of their own, which is esoteric and jealously guarded. Their pride gave rise a year or two ago to an amusing strike at the People's Theater. The actors of the three Yiddish companies in New York are normally paid on the share rather than the salary system. In the case of the company now at the People's Theater, this system proved very profitable. The star actors, Jacob Adler and Boris Thomashevsky, and their wives, who are actresses (Mrs. Adler being the heavy realistic tragedienne and Mrs. Thomashevsky the star soubrette) have probably received on an average during that time as much as a hundred and twenty-five dollars a week for each couple. But they, with Mr. Edelstein, the businessman, are lessees of the theater, run the risk, and pay the expenses, which are not small. The rent of the theater is twenty thousand dollars a year, and the weekly expenses, besides, amount to about eleven hundred dollars. The subordinate actors, who risk nothing, since they do not share the expenses, have made amounts during this favorable period ranging from fourteen dollars a week on the average for the poorest actors to seventy-five dollars for those just beneath the stars. But, in spite of what is exceedingly good pay in the Bowery, the actors of this theater formed a union, and struck for wages instead of shares. This however, was only an incidental feature. The real cause was that the management of the theater, with the energetic Thomashevsky at the head, insisted that the actors should be prompt at rehearsals, and if they were not, indulged in unseemly epithets. The actors' pride was aroused, and the union was formed to insure their ease and dignity and to protect them from harsh words. The management imported actors from Chicago. Several of the actors here stood by their employers, notably Miss Weinblatt, a popular young ingenue, who, on account of her great memory is called "the Yiddish encyclopedia," and Miss Gudinski, an actress of commanding presence. Miss Weinblatt forced her father, once an actor, now a farmer, into the service of the management. But the actors easily triumphed. Misses Gudinski and Weinblatt were forced to join the union, Mr. Weinblatt returned to his farm, the scabs were packed off to Philadelphia, and the wage system was introduced. A delegation was sent to Philadelphia to throw cabbages at the new actors, who appeared in the Yiddish performances in that city. The triumphant actors now receive on the average probably ten to fifteen dollars a week less than under the old system. Mr. Conrad, who began the disaffection, receives a salary of twenty-nine dollars a week, fully ten dollars less than he received for months before the strike. But the dignity of the Yiddish actor is now placed beyond assault. As one of them recently said, "We shall no longer be spat upon nor called dog."

The Yiddish actor is so supreme that until recently a regular system of hazing playwrights was in vogue. Joseph Latteiner and Professor M. Horowitz were long recognized as the only legitimate ghetto playwrights. When a new writer came to the theater with a manuscript, various were the pranks the actors would play. They would induce him to try on, one after another, all the costumes in the house, in order to help him conceive the characters; or they would make him spout the play from the middle of the stage, they themselves retiring to the gallery to "see how it sounded." In the midst of his exertions they would slip away, and he would find himself shouting to the empty boards. Or, in the midst of a mock rehearsal, some actor would shout, "He is coming, the great Professor Horowitz, and he will eat you"; and they would rush from the theater with the panic-stricken playwright following close at their heels.

The supremacy of the Yiddish actor has, however, its humorous limitations. The Orthodox Jews who go to the theater on Friday night, the beginning of Sabbath, are commonly somewhat ashamed of themselves and try to quiet their consciences by a vociferous condemnation of the actions on the stage. The actor, who through the exigencies of his role, is compelled to appear on Friday night with a cigar in his mouth, is frequently greeted with hisses and strenuous cries of "Shame, shame, smoke on the Sabbath!" from the proletarian hypocrites in the gallery.

The plays at these theaters vary in a general way with the varying audiences of which I have spoken above. The thinking socialists naturally select a less violent play than the comparatively illogical anarchists. Societies of relatively conservative Jews desire a historical play in which the religious Hebrew in relation to the persecuting Christian is put in pathetic

*Yiddish playwrights*

and melodramatic situations. There are a very large number of "culture" pieces produced, which, roughly speaking, are plays in which the difference between the Jew of one generation and the next is dramatically portrayed. The pathos or tragedy involved in differences of faith and point of view between the old rabbi and his more enlightened children is expressed in many historical plays of the general character of *Uriel Acosta*, though in less lasting form. Such plays, however, are called historical plunder by that very up-to-date element of the intellectual ghetto which is dominated by the Russian spirit of realism. It is the demand of these fierce realists that of late years has produced a supply of theatrical productions attempting to present a faithful picture of the actual conditions of life. Permeating all these kinds of plays is the amusement instinct pure and simple. For the benefit of the crowd of ignorant people grotesque humor, popular songs, vaudeville tricks, are inserted everywhere.

Of these plays the realistic are of the most value, for they often give the actual ghetto life with surprising strength and fidelity. The past three years have been their great seasons, and have developed a large crop of new playwrights, mainly journalists who write miscellaneous articles for the East Side newspapers. Jacob Gordin, of whom we shall have frequent occasion to speak, has been writing plays for several years, and was the first realistic playwright; he remains the strongest and most prominent in this kind of play. Professor Horowitz, who is now the lessee of the Windsor Theater, situated on the Bowery, between Grand and Canal streets, represents, along with Joseph Latteiner, the conservative and traditional aspects of the stage. He is an interesting man, fifty-six years of age, and has been connected with the Yiddish stage practically since its origin. His father was a teacher in a Hebrew school, and he himself is a man of uncommon learning. He has made a great study of the stage, has written one hundred and sixty-seven plays, and claims to be an authority on dramaturgy. Latteiner is equally productive, but few of their plays are anything more than Yiddish adaptations of old operas and melodramas in other languages. Long runs are impossible on the Yiddish stage, and consequently the playwrights produce many plays and are not very scrupulous in their methods. The absence of dramatic criticism and the ignorance of the audience enable them to crib with impunity. As one of the actors said, Latteiner and Horowitz and their class took their first plays from some foreign source and since then have been repeating themselves. The actor said that when he is cast in a Latteiner play he does not need to learn his part. He needs only to understand the general situation; the character and the words he already knows from having appeared in many other Latteiner plays.

The professor, nevertheless, naturally regards himself and Latteiner as the real Yiddish playwrights. For many years after the first bands of actors reached the New York ghetto these two men held undisputed sway. Latteiner leaned to "romantic," Horowitz to "culture," plays, and both used material which was mainly historical. The professor regards that as the bright period of the ghetto stage. Since then there has been, in his opinion, a decadence which began with the translation of the classics into Yiddish. *Hamlet, Othello, King Lear,* and plays of Schiller, were put upon the stage and are still being performed. Sometimes they are almost literally translated, sometimes adapted until they are realistic representations of Jewish life. Gordin's *Jewish King Lear,* for instance, represents Shakespeare's idea only in the most general way, and weaves about it a sordid story of Jewish character and life. Of *Hamlet* there are two versions, one adapted, in which Shakespeare's idea is reduced to a ludicrous shadow, the interest lying entirely in the presentation of Jewish customs.

The first act of the Yiddish version represents the wedding feast of Hamlet's mother and uncle. In the Yiddish play the uncle is a rabbi in a small village in Russia. He did not poison Hamlet's father but broke the latter's heart by wooing and winning his queen. Hamlet is off somewhere getting educated as a rabbi. While he is gone his father dies. Six weeks afterward the son returns in the midst of the wedding feast and turns the feast into a funeral. Scenes of rant follow between mother and son, Ophelia and Hamlet, interspersed with jokes and sneers at the sect of rabbis who think they communicate with the angels. The wicked rabbi conspires against Hamlet, trying to make him out a nihilist. The plot is discovered and the wicked rabbi is sent to Siberia. The last act is the graveyard scene. It is snowing violently. The grave is near a huge windmill. Ophelia is brought in on the bier. Hamlet mourns by her side and is married, according to the Jewish custom, to the dead woman. Then he dies of a broken heart. The other version is almost a literal translation. To these translations of the classics, Professor Horowitz objects on the ground that the ignorant Yiddish public cannot understand them, because what learning they have is limited to distinctively Yiddish subjects and traditions.

Another important step in what the professor calls the degeneration of the stage was the introduction a few years ago of the American pistol play—meaning the fierce melodrama which has been for so long a characteristic of the English plays produced on the Bowery.

But what has contributed more than anything else to what the good man calls the present deplorable condition of the theater was the advent of realism. "It was then," said the professor one day with calm indignation, "that the genuine Yiddish play was persecuted. Young writers came from Russia and swamped the ghetto with scurrilous attacks on me and Latteiner. No number of the newspaper appeared that did not contain a scathing criticism. They did not object to the actors, who in reality were very bad, but it was the play they aimed at. These writers knew nothing about dramaturgy, but their heads were filled with senseless realism. Anything historical and distinctively Yiddish they thought bad. For a long time Latteiner and I were able to keep their realistic plays off the boards, but for the last few years there has been an open field for everybody.

The result is that horrors under the mask of realism have been put upon the stage. This year is the worst of all—characters butchered on the stage, the coarsest language, the most revolting situations, without ideas, with no real material. It cannot last, however. Latteiner and I continue with our real Yiddish plays, and we shall yet regain entire possession of the field."

At least this much may fairly be conceded to Professor Horowitz—that the realistic writers in what is in reality an excellent attempt often go to excess, and are often unskillful as far as stage construction is concerned. In the reaction from plays with "pleasant" endings, they tend to prefer equally unreal "unpleasant" endings—onion plays, as the opponents of the realists call them. They, however, have written a number of plays which are distinctively of the New York ghetto and which attempt an unsentimental presentation of truth. Professor Horowitz's plays, on the contrary, are largely based upon the sentimental representation of inexact Jewish history. They herald the glory and wrongs of the Hebrew people, and are badly constructed melodramas of conventional character. Another class of plays written by Professor Horowitz, and which have occasionally great but temporary prosperity, are what he calls *Zeitstücke*. Some American newspaper sensation is rapidly dramatized and put hot on the boards, such as *Marie Barberi, Dr. Buchanan,* and *Dr. Harris.*

The three theaters—the People's, the Windsor, and the Thalia (which is on the Bowery opposite the Windsor) are in a general way very similar in the character of the plays produced, in the standard of acting, and in the character of the audience. There are, however, some minor differences. The People's is the "swellest" and probably the least characteristic of the three. It panders to the "uptown" element of the ghetto, to the downtown tradesman who is beginning to climb a little. The baleful influence in art of the nouveaux riches has at this house its ghetto expression. There is a tendency there to imitate the showy qualities of the Broadway theaters—melodrama, farce, scenery, etc. No babies are admitted, and the house is exceedingly clean in comparison with the theaters farther down the Bowery. Three years ago this company was at the Windsor Theater, and made so much money that they hired the People's—that old home of Irish-American melodrama; and this atmosphere seems slightly to have affected the Yiddish productions. Magnificent performances quite out of the line of the best ghetto drama have been attempted, notably Yiddish dramatizations of successful uptown productions. Hauptmann's *Versunkene Glocke, Sapho, Quo Vadis,* and other popular Broadway plays in flimsy adaptations were tried with little success, as the Yiddish audiences hardly felt themselves at home in these unfamiliar scenes and settings.

The best trained of the three companies is at present that of the Thalia Theater. Here many excellent realistic plays are given. Of late years, the great playwright of the colony, Jacob Gordin, has written mainly for this theater. There, too, is the best of the younger actresses, Mrs. Bertha Kalisch. She is the prettiest woman on the ghetto stage and was at one time the leading lady of the Imperial Theater at Bucharest. She takes the leading woman parts in plays like *Fedora, Magda,* and *The Jewish Zaza.* The principal actor at this theater is David Kessler, who is one of the best of the ghetto actors in realistic parts, and one of the worst when cast, as he often is, as the romantic lover. The actor of most prominence among the younger men is Mr. Moshkovitch, who hopes to be a star and one of the management. When the union was formed he was in a quandary. Should he join or should he not? He feared it might be a bad prece-

*Mr. Moshkovitz*

dent, which the actors would use against him when he became a star. And he did not want to get them down on him. So before he joined, he entered solemn protests at all the cafés on Canal Street. The strike, he maintained, was unnecessary. The actors were well-paid and well-treated. Discipline should be maintained. But he would join because of his universal sympathy with actors and with the poor—as a matter of sentiment merely, against his better judgment.

The company at the Windsor is the weakest, so far as acting is concerned, of the three. Very few realistic plays are given there, for Professor Horowitz is the lessee, and he prefers the historical Jewish opera and culture plays. Besides, the company is not strong enough to undertake successfully many new productions, although it includes some good actors. Here Mrs. Prager vies as a prima donna with Mrs. Karb of the People's and Mrs. Kalisch of the Thalia. Professor Horowitz thinks she is far better than the other two. As he puts it, there are two and a half prima donnas in the ghetto—at the Windsor Theater there is a complete one, leaving one and a half between the People's and the Thalia. Jacob Adler of the People's, the professor thinks, is no actor, only a remarkable caricaturist. As Adler is the most noteworthy representative of the realistic actors of the ghetto, the professor's opinion shows what the traditional Yiddish playwright thinks of realism. The strong realistic playwright, Jacob Gordin, the professor admits, has a "biting" dialogue and "unconsciously writes good cultural plays, which he calls realistic, but his realistic plays, properly speaking, are bad caricatures of life."

The managers and actors of the three theaters criticize one another indeed with charming directness, and they all have their followers in the ghetto and their special cafés on Grand or Canal streets, where their particular prejudices are sympathetically expressed. The actors and lessees of the People's are proud of their fine theater, proud that no babies are brought there. There is a great dispute between the supporters of this theater and those of the Thalia as to which is the stronger company and which produces the most realistic plays. The manager of the Thalia maintains that the People's is sensational, and that his theater alone represents true realism; while the supporter of the People's points scornfully to the large number of operas produced at the Thalia. They both unite in condemning the Windsor, Professor Horowitz's theater, as producing no new plays and as hopelessly behind the times, "full of historical plunder." An episode in *The Ragpicker of Paris,* played at the Windsor when the present People's company were there, amusingly illustrates the jealousy which exists between the companies. An old beggar is picking over a heap of moth-eaten, coverless books, some of which he keeps and some rejects. He comes across two versions of a play, *The Two Vagrants,* one of which was used at the Thalia and the other at the Windsor. The version used at the Windsor receives the beggar's commendation, and the other is thrown in a contemptuous manner into a dust heap.

*Jacob Adler*

## REALISM, THE SPIRIT OF THE GHETTO THEATER

The distinctive thing about the intellectual and artistic life of the Russian Jews of the New York ghetto, the spirit of realism, is noticeable even on the popular stage. The most interesting plays are those in which the realistic spirit predominates, and the best among the actors and playwrights are the realists. The realistic element, too, is the latest one in the history of the Yiddish stage. The Jewish theaters in other parts of the world, which, compared with the three in New York, are unorganized, present only anachronistic and fantastic historical and biblical plays, or comic opera with vaudeville specialties attached. These things, as we have said in the last section, are, to be sure, given in the Yiddish theaters on the Bowery too, but there are also plays which in part at least portray the customs and problems of the ghetto community, and are of comparatively recent origin.

There are two men connected with the ghetto stage who particularly express the distinctive realism of the intellectual East Side—Jacob Adler, one of the two best actors, and Jacob Gordin, the playwright. Adler, a man of great energy, tried for many years to make a theater succeed on the Bowery which should give only what he called good plays. Gordin's dramas, with a few exceptions, were the only plays on contemporary life which Adler thought worthy of presentation. The attempt to give exclusively realistic art, which is the only art on the Bowery, failed.

*Jacob Gordin*

There, in spite of the widespread feeling for realism, the mass of the people desire to be amused and are bored by anything with the form of art. So now Adler is connected with the People's Theater, which gives all sorts of shows, from Gordin's plays to ludicrous history, frivolous comic opera, and conventional melodrama. But Adler acts for the most part only in the better sort. He is an actor of unusual power and vividness. Indeed, in his case, as in that of some other Bowery actors, it is only the Yiddish dialect which stands between him and the distinction of a wide reputation.

In almost every play given on the Bowery all the elements are represented. Vaudeville, history, realism, comic opera, are generally mixed together. Even in the plays of Gordin there are clownish and operatic intrusions, inserted as a conscious condition of success. On the other hand, even in the distinctively formless plays, in comic opera and melodrama, there are striking illustrations of the popular feeling for realism—bits of dialogue, happy strokes of characterization of well-known ghetto types, sordid scenes faithful to the life of the people.

It is the acting which gives even to the plays having no intrinsic relation to reality a frequent quality of naturalness. The Yiddish players, even the poorer among them, act with remarkable sincerity. Entirely lacking in self-consciousness, they attain almost from the outset to a direct and forcible expressiveness. They, like the audience, rejoice in what they deem the truth. In the general lack of really good plays they yet succeed in introducing the note of realism. To be true to nature is their strongest passion, and even in a conventional melodrama their sincerity, or their characterization in the comic episodes, often redeems the play from utter barrenness.

And the little touches of truth to the life of the people are thoroughly appreciated by the audience—much more generally so than in the case of the better plays, where there is more or less strictness of form and intellectual intention, difficult for the untutored crowd to understand. In the "easy" plays, it is the realistic touches which tell most. The spectators laugh at the exact reproduction by the actor of a tattered type which they know well. A scene of perfect sordidness will arouse the sympathetic laughter or tears of the people. "It is so natural," they say to one another, "so true." The word natural indeed is the favorite term of praise in the ghetto. What hits home to them, to their sense of humor or of sad fact, is sure to move, although sometimes in a manner surprising to a visitor. To what seems to him very sordid and sad they will frequently respond with laughter.

One of the most beloved actors in the ghetto is Zelig Mogalesco, now at the People's Theater, a comedian of natural talent and of the most felicitous instinct for characterization. Unlike the strenuous Adler, he has no ideas about realism or anything else. He acts in any kind of play, and could not tell the difference between truth and burlesque caricature. And yet he is remarkable for his naturalness, and popular because of it. Adler with his ideas is sometimes too serious for the people, but Mogalesco's naive fidelity to reality always meets with the sympathy of a simple audience loving the homely and unpretentious truth. About Adler, strong actor that he is, and also about the talented Gordin, there is something of the doctrinaire.

But, although the best actors of the three Yiddish theaters in the ghetto are realists by instinct and training, the thoroughly frivolous element in the plays has its prominent interpreters. Joseph Latteiner is the most popular playwright in the Bowery, and Boris Thomashevsky perhaps the most popular actor. Latteiner has written over a hundred plays, no one of which has form or ideas. He calls them *Volksstücke* (plays of the people), and naively admits that he writes directly to the demand. They are mainly mixed melodrama, broad burlesque, and comic opera. His heroes are all intended for Boris Thomashevsky, a young man, fat, with curling black hair, languorous eyes, and a rather effeminate voice, who is thought very beautiful by the girls of the ghetto. Thomashevsky has a face with no mimic capacity, and a temperament absolutely impervious to mood or feeling. But he picturesquely stands in the middle of the stage and declaims phlegmatically the role of the hero, and satisfies the "Romantic" demand of the audience. Nothing could show more clearly how much more genuine the feeling of the ghetto is for fidelity to life than for romantic fancy. How small a part of the grace and charm of life the Yiddish audiences enjoy may be judged by the fact that the romantic appeal of a Thomashevsky is eminently satisfying to them. Girls and men from the sweatshops, a large part of such an audience, are moved by a very crude attempt at beauty. On the other hand they are so familiar with sordid fact, that the theatrical representation of it must be relatively excellent. Therefore the art of the ghetto, theatrical and other, is deeply and painfully realistic.

When we turn to Jacob Gordin's plays, to other plays of similar character and to the audiences to which they specifically appeal, we have realism worked out consciously in art, the desire to express life as it is, and at the same time the frequent expression of revolt against the reality of things, and particularly against the actual system of society. Consequently the problem play has its representation in the ghetto. It presents the hideous conditions of life in the ghetto—the poverty, the sordid constant reference to money, the immediate sensuality, the jocular callousness—and underlying the mere statement of the facts an intellectual and passionate revolt.

The thinking element of the ghetto is largly socialistic, and the socialists flock to the theater the nights when the Gordin type of play is produced. They discuss the meaning and justice of the play between the acts, and after the performance repair to the Canal Street cafés to continue their serious discourse. The unthinking nihilists are also represented, but not so frequently at the best plays as at productions in which are found crude and screaming condemnation of existing conditions. The anarchistic propaganda hired the Windsor Theater for the establishment of a fund to start the *Freie Arbeiter-stimme*, an anarchistic newspaper. *The Beggar of Odessa* was the play selected—an adaptation of *The Ragpicker of Paris*, a play by Felix Piot, the anarchistic agitator of the French Commune in 1871. The features of the play particularly interesting to the audience were those emphasizing the clashing of social classes. The old ragpicker, a model man, clever, brilliant, and good, is a philosopher too, and says many things warmly welcomed by the audience. As he picks up his rags he sings about how even the clothing of the great comes but to dust. His adopted daughter is poor, and consequently noble and sweet. The villains are all rich; all the very poor characters are good. Another play, *Vogele*, is partly a satire of the rich Jew by the poor Jew. "The rich Jews," sang the comedian, "toil not, neither do they spin. They work not, they suffer not—why then do they live on this earth?" This unthinking revolt is the opposite pole to the unthinking vaudeville and melodrama. In many of the plays referred to roughly as of the Gordin-Adler type—although they were not all written by Gordin nor played by Adler—we find a realism more true in feeling and cast in stronger dramatic form. In some of these plays there is no problem element; in few is that element so prominent as essentially to interfere with the character of the play as a presentation of life.

One of the plays most characteristic, as at once presenting the life of the ghetto and suggesting its problems, is *Minna*, the drama about the Yiddish Nora. Although the general idea of Ibsen's *Doll's House* is taken, the atmosphere and life are original. The first scene represents the house of a poor Jewish laborer on the East Side. His wife and daughter are dressing to go to see *A Doll's House* with the boarder —a young man whom they have been forced to take into the house because of their poverty. He is full of ideas and philosophy, and the two women fall in love with him, and give him all the good things to eat. When the laborer returns from his hard day's work, he finds that there is nothing to eat, and that his wife and daugher are going to the play with the boarder. The women despise the poor man, who is fit only to work, eat, and sleep. The wife philosophizes on the atrocity of marrying a man without intellectual interests, and finally drinks carbolic acid. This Ibsen idea is set in a picture rich with realistic detail: the dialect, the poverty, the types of character, the humor of Yiddish New York. Jacob Adler plays the husband, and displays a vivid imagination for details calculated to bring out the man's beseeching bestiality: his filthy manners, his physical ailments, his greed, the quickness of his anger and of resulting pacification. Like most of the realistic plays of the ghetto, *Minna* is a genuine play of manners. It has a general idea and presents also the setting and characters of reality.

*The Slaughter*, written by Gordin, and with the main masculine character taken by David Kessler, an actor of occasionally great realistic strength, is the story of the symbolic murder of a fragile young girl by her parents, who force her to marry a rich man who has all the vices and whom she hates. The picture of the poorhouse, of the old mother and father and half-witted stepson with whom the girl is

*David Kessler*

unconsciously in love, in its faithfulness to life is typical of scenes in many of these plays. It is rich in character and milieu drawing. There is another scene of miserable life in the second act. The girl is married and living with the rich brute. In the same house is his mistress, curt and cold, and two children by a former wife. The old parents come to see the wife; she meets them with the joy of starved affection. But the husband enters and changes the scene to one of hate and violence. The old mother tells him, however, of the heir that is to come. Then there is a superb scene of naive joy in the midst of all the sordid gloom. There is rapturous delight of the old people, turbulent triumph of the husband, and satisfaction of the young wife. They make a holiday of it. Wine is brought. They all love one another for the time. The scene is representative of the way the poor Jews welcome their offspring. But indescribable violence and abuse follow, and the wife finally kills her husband, in a scene where realism riots into burlesque, as it frequently does on the Yiddish stage.

But for absolute, intense realism Gordin's *Wild Man*, unrelieved by a problem idea, is unrivaled. An idiot boy falls in love with his stepmother without knowing what love is. He is abused by his father and brother, beaten on account of his ineptitudes. His sister and another brother take his side, and the two camps revile each other in unmistakable language. The father marries again; his new wife is a heartless, faithless woman, and she and the daughter quarrel. After repeated scenes of brutality to the idiot, the daughter is driven out to make her own living. Adler's portraiture of the idiot is a great bit of technical acting. The poor fellow is filled with the mysterious wonderings of an incapable mind. His shadow terrifies and interests him. He philosophizes about life and death. He is puzzled and worried by everything; the slightest sound preys on him. Physically alert, his senses serve only to trouble and terrify the mind which cannot interpret what they present. The burlesque which Mr. Adler puts into the part was inserted to please the crowd, but increases the horror of it, as when Lear went mad; for the Elizabethan audiences laughed and had their souls wrung at the same time. The idiot ludicrously describes his growing love. In pantomime he tells a long story. It is evident, even without words, that he is constructing a complicated symbolism to express what he does not know. He falls into epilepsy and joins stiffly in the riotous dance. The play ends so fearfully that it shades into mere burlesque.

This horrible element in so many of these plays marks the point where realism passes into fantastic sensationalism. The facts of life in the ghetto are in themselves unpleasant, and consequently it is natural that a dramatic exaggeration of them results in something poignantly disagreeable. The intense seriousness of the Russian Jew, which accounts for what is excellent in these plays, explains also the rasping falseness of the extreme situations. It is a curious fact that idiots, often introduced in the Yiddish plays, amuse the Jewish audience as much as they used to the Elizabethan mob.

One of the most skillful of Gordin's Yiddish adap-

tations is *The Oath,* founded on Gerhart Hauptmann's *Fuhrmann Henschel.* In the first act a dying
peasant is exhibited on the stage. In Hauptmann's
play it is a woman; in Gordin's, it is a man. He is
racked with coughing. A servant clatters over the
floor with her heavy boots; another servant feeds the
sick man from a coarse bowl; and the steward works
at the household accounts. The dying man's wife,
and their little boy, enter, and its is apparent that
something has been going on between her and the
steward. They and the servants dine realistically and
coarsely and neglect the dying man. When they
leave, the dying man teaches his son how to say *Kaddish* for his soul when he is dead. When he dies he
makes his wife swear that she will never marry
again. In the second act she is about to marry the
steward, and the Jewish customs are here used, as is
often the case with the Yiddish playwright, to inten-
sify the dramatic effect of a scene. It is just a year
from the time of her husband's death, and the candles are burning, therefore, on the table. According
to the Orthodox belief the soul of the dead is present
when the candles burn. The little boy, feeling that
his mother is about to marry again, blows out the
candles. The mother, horror-stricken, rushes to him
and asks him why he did it. "I did not want my father
to see that you are going to marry again," says the
little fellow. It was an affecting scene and left few
dry eyes in the audience.

At the beginning of the third act the wife and
servant are living together, married. He comes on
the stage, sleepy, brutal, calling loudly for a drink,

abuses the little boy and quarrels with his wife; he is a crude, dishonorable, coarse brute. He drives away a faithful servant and returns to his swinish slumber. An old couple (the woman being the sister of the dead man), who are always torturing the wife with having broken her vow, hint to her that her new husband is too attentive to the maid servant. She is angry and incredulous, and calls the maid to her, but when she sees her in the doorway, before a word is spoken, she realizes it is true, and sends her away. The husband enters and she passionately taxes him. He admits it, but justifies himself: he is young, a high-liver, etc., why shouldn't he? Just then the child is brought in—he has been drowned in the river nearby.

In the beginning of the fourth and last act the husband again appears as a riotous, jovial fellow. He has played a joke and turned a driver out of his cart, and he nearly splits his sides with merriment. Drunk, he admirably sings a song and dances. His wife enters. She hears her vow repeated by the winds, by the trees, everywhere. Her dead child haunts her. Her husband has stolen and misspent their money. She talks with the faithful servant about the maid's baby. She wanders about at night, unable to sleep. Her brute husband calls to her from the house, saying he is afraid to sleep alone. Another talk ensues between them. He asks her why she is old so soon. She burns the house and herself, the neighbors rush in, and the play is over.

Some of the more striking of the realistic plays on the ghetto stage have been partly described, but realism in the details of character and setting appears in all of them, even in comic opera and melodrama. In many the element of revolt, even if it is not the basis of the play, is expressed in occasional dialogues. Burlesque runs through them all, but burlesque, after all, is a comment on the facts of life. And all these points are emphasized and driven home by sincere and forcible acting.

Crude in form as these plays are, and unpleasant as they often are in subject and in the life portrayed, they are yet refreshing to persons who have been bored by the empty farce and inane cheerfulness of the uptown theaters.

## THE HISTORY OF THE YIDDISH STAGE

The Yiddish stage, founded in Rumania in 1876 by Abraham Goldfaden, has reached its highest development in the city of New York, where there are seventy or eighty professional actors; not far from a dozen playwrights, of whom three have written collectively more than three hundred plays; dramas on almost every subject, produced on the inspiration of various schools of dramatic art; and an enormous Russian-Jewish colony, which fills the theaters and creates so strong a demand that the stage responds with a distinctive, complete, and interesting popular art.

The best actor now in the ghetto, with one exception, was in the original company. That exception, with the help of a realistic playwright introduced an important element in the development of the stage. With the lives of these three men the history of the Yiddish stage is intimately connected. The first actor was a singer in the synagogue of Bucharest, the first playwright a composer of Yiddish songs. The foundation of the Yiddish stage might therefore be said to lie in the Bucharest synagogue and the popular music-hall performance.

Zelig Mogalesco, the best comedian in the New York ghetto, has seen, although not quite forty years of age, the birth of the Yiddish stage and may survive its death. He was born in Koloraush, a town in the province of Bessarabia, near Rumania. His father was a poor shopkeeper, and Mogalesco never went to school. But he was endowed by nature with a remarkable voice and ear and composed music with easy felicity. The population of the town was Orthodox Jewish, and consequently no theater was allowed. It was therefore in the synagogue that the musical appetite of the Jews found satisfaction. It was the habit of the poor people to hire as inexpensive a cantor as possible, and this cantor might very well be ignorant of everything except singing. Yet these cantors were so popular that the famous ones traveled from town to town, in much the same way that the visiting German actor (*Gast*) does today, and sometimes charged admission fees.

When Mogalesco was nine years old, Nissy of the town of Bells, the most famous cantor in southern Russia, visited Mogalesco's town. The boy's friends urged him to visit the great man and display his voice. Little Mogalesco, with his mezzosoprano, went to the inn, and Nissy was astounded. "My dear boy," he said, "go home and fetch your parents." With them the cantor signed a contract by which Zelig was bound to him as a kind of musical apprentice for three years. The boy was to receive, in addition to his board and clothing, five rubles the first year, ten the second, and fifteen the third—fifteen dollars for the three years.

Soon Mogalesco became widely known among the cantors of southern Russia. In six months he could read music so well that they called him "little Zelig, the music eater." At the end of the first year the leading cantor of Bucharest, Israel Kupfer (who, by the way, has been cantor in a New York synagogue of the East Side) went to Russia to secure the services of Mogalesco. To avoid the penalties of a broken contract, Kupfer hurried with little Zelig to Rumania, and the boy remained in Bucharest for several years. At the age of fourteen he conducted a choir of twenty men under Kupfer. He also became director of the chorus in the Gentile opera. While there he began "to burn," as he expressed it, with a desire to go on the stage, but the Gentiles would not admit the talented Jew.

It was when Mogalesco was about twenty years old that the Yiddish stage was born. In 1876 or 1877, Abraham Goldfaden went to Bucharest. This man had formerly been a successful merchant in Russia, but had failed. He was a poet, and to make a living he called that art into play. In Russia he had written many Yiddish songs, set them to music, and sung them in private. In the society in which he lived he deemed that beneath his dignity, but when he lost his money he went to Bucharest and there on the stage sang his own poems, the music for which he took from many sources. He became a kind of music-hall performer but did not long remain satisfied with this modest art. His dissatisfaction led him to create what later developed into the present Yiddish theater. The Talmud prohibited the stage, but at the time when Goldfaden was casting about for something to do worthy of his genius, the gymnasiums were thrown open to the Jews, and the result was a more tolerant spirit. Therefore, Goldfaden decided to found a Yiddish theater. He went to Kupfer, the cantor, and Kupfer recommended Mogalesco as an actor for the new company. Goldfaden saw the young man act, and the comedy genius of Mogalesco helped in the initial idea of a Yiddish play. Mogalesco at first refused to enter into the scheme. A Yiddish drama seemed too narrow to him, for he aspired to the Christian stage. But when Goldfaden offered to adopt him and teach him the Gentile languages, Mogalesco agreed and became the first Yiddish actor. Other singers in Kupfer's choir also joined Goldfaden's company.

Thus the foundation of the Yiddish stage lay in the Bucharest synagogue. The beginnings, of course, were small. Several other actors were secured, among them Moses Silbermann, who is still acting on the New York ghetto stage. No girls could at that time be obtained for the stage, for it is against the Talmudic Law for a man even to hear a girl sing, and men consequently played females roles, as in Elizabethan times in England. The first play that Goldfaden wrote was *The Grandmother and Her Grandchild*, the second was *Der Shmendrik*, and Mogalesco played the grandmother in one and a little spoiled boy in the other. His success in both was enormous, and he still enacts on the Bowery the part of the little boy. The first performances of Goldfaden's play were given in Bucharest at the time of the Russian-Turkish war, and the city was filled with Russian contractors and workmen. They overcrowded the theater and applauded Mogalesco to the echo. From that time the success of the Yiddish stage was assured. Goldfaden tried to get a permit to act in Russia, without success at first; but he played in Odessa without a license, in a secret way, and in the end a permit was secured. Other Yiddish companies sprang up. Girls were admitted to the chorus, and women began to play female roles. The first woman on the Yiddish stage was a girl who is now Mrs. Karb, and who may be seen in the Yiddish company at present in the People's Theater on the Bowery. She is the best liked of all the ghetto's actresses, has been a sweet singer, and is now an actress of considerable distinction. In Bucharest, before she went on the stage, she was a tailor girl and used to sing in the shop. She appeared in 1878 in *The Evil Eye,* and made an immediate hit. That was the third Yiddish play, and, in the absence of Goldfaden, it was written by Joseph Latteiner, who (with the possible exception of Professor Horowitz, who began to write about the same time) was for many years the most popular playwright in the New York ghetto.

In 1884 the Yiddish theater was forbidden in Russia. It was supposed by the government to be a hot-bed of political plots, but some of the Yiddish actors think that the jealousy of Gentile actors was responsible for this idea. Two years before there had been a transmigration of Russian and Rumanian Jews to America on a large scale. Therefore the players banished from Russia had a refuge and an audience in New York. In 1884 the first Yiddish company came to this country. It was not Goldfaden's or Mogalesco's company, but one formed after them. In it were actors who still act in New York—Moses Heine, Moses Silbermann, Mrs. Karb, and Latteiner the playwright.

The first Yiddish theater was called the Oriental. It was a music hall on the Bowery, transformed for the purpose. A year later Mogalesco, Kessler, Professor Horowitz, and their company came to New York and opened the Rumania Theater. From that time they changed theaters frequently. It is worthy of note that with one exception the actors identified with the beginnings of the Yiddish stage are still the best.

That exception is Jacob Adler, who, not counting Mogalesco, is the best actor in the ghetto. They are both character actors, but Mogalesco is essentially a comedian, while Adler plays roles ranging from burlesque to tragedy. Mogalesco is a natural genius, with a spontaneity superior to that of Adler, but he has no general education nor intellectual life. But the forcible Adler, a man of great energy, a fighter, is filled with one great idea, which is almost a passion with him, and which has marked a development in the

Yiddish theater. To be natural, to be real, to express the actual life of the people, with serious intent, is what Jacob Adler stands for. Up to the time when he appeared on the scene in New York there had been no serious plays acted on the Yiddish stage. Comic opera, lurid melodrama, adaptations and translations, historical plays representing the traditions of the Jews, were exclusively the thing. Through the acting, indeed, which on the Yiddish stage is constantly animated by the desire for sincerity and naturalness, the real life of the people was constantly suggested in some part of the play. When Mogalesco took a comic part, he would interpolate phrases and actions, suggesting that life, which he instinctively and spontaneously knew, and it was so with the other actors also. But this element was accidental and fragmentary previous to the coming of Jacob Adler.

Until then Latteiner and Professor Horowitz, the authors of the first historical plays of the Yiddish stage, and still the most popular playwrights in the ghetto, held almost undisputed sway.

Joseph Latteiner, of whom brief mention has already been made, represents thoroughly the strong commercial spirit of the Yiddish stage. He writes with but one thought—to please the mass of the people—writes "easy plays," to quote his own words. His plays, therefore, are the very spirit of formlessness—burlesque, popularly vulgar jokes, flat heroism combined about the flimsiest dramatic structure. He is the type of the businessman of the ghetto. Although successful, he lives in an unpleasant tenement, and seems much poorer than he really is. He has an unemphatic, conciliatory manner of talking, and everything he says is discouragingly practical. He is a Rumanian Jew, forty-six years of age. His parents intended him for a rabbi, but he was too poor to reach the goal, although he learned several languages. These afterward stood him in good stead, for he often translates and adapts plays for the Bowery stage. Unable to be a rabbi, Latteiner cast about for a means of making his living. As a boy he was not interested in the stage, but one day he saw a German play in one act and thought he could adapt it with music to the Yiddish stage. It was successful, and Latteiner, as he put it, "discovered himself." He has since written over a hundred plays, and is engaged by the company at the Thalia Theater as the regular playwright. He calls himself *Volksdichter*, and maintains that his plays improve with the taste of the people, but this statement is open to considerable doubt.

In speaking of the popular playwright, and the purely commercial character and consequent formlessness of the plays before the appearance of Adler, important mention should be made of Boris Thomashevsky, already briefly referred to as the idol of the Jewish matinee girls. He is the most popular actor on the Yiddish stage, and for him Latteiner particularly writes. Thomashevsky is a large fat man, with expressionless features and curly black hair, which he arranges in leonine forms. He generally appears as the hero, and is a successful though a rather listless barnstormer. The more intelligent of his audience are inclined to smile at Mr. Thomashevsky's talent in romantic parts, of the reality of which, however, he, with a large section of the community, is very firmly convinced. In fairness, however, it should be said that when Mr. Thomashevsky occasionally leaves the role of hero for an unsentimental character, particularly one which expresses supercilious superiority, he is excellent. As time goes on he will probably take less and less the romantic lead and grow more and more satisfactory. He is the youngest of the prominent actors of the Bowery. Before the coming of Heine's company in 1884, he was a pretty little boy in the ghetto, who used to play female roles in amateur theatricals. But when the professionals came, he was eclipsed and went out of sight for some time. He grew to be a handsome man, however; his voice changed, and, with the help of a very different man, Jacob Adler, Thomashevsky found an important place on the Yiddish stage. He and Adler are now the leading actors of the People's Theater, but they never appear together, Thomashevsky being the main interpreter of the plays which appeal distinctively to the rabble, and Adler of those which form the really original Yiddish drama of a serious nature.

Jacob Adler was born in Odessa, Russia, in 1855, of middle-class parents. He went to the public school, but was very slow to learn, and was treated roughly by his teachers, whose favorite weapon was a ruler of thorns. School, therefore, as he says, "made a bad impression" on him, and he left it for business, but got along as badly there, not being able to brook the brutally expressed authority of his masters. But while he passed rapidly from one firm to another, through the kindness of a wealthy uncle he was able to cut a swell figure in Odessa, and became a dandy and something of a lady killer. He was then only eighteen, but the serious ideas which at a later time he strenuously sought to bring into prominence in New York already began to assert themselves. Then there was no Yiddish theater, but of the Gentile Russian theater in Odessa he was very fond. The serious realistic Russian play was what particularly took his fancy. The Russian tragedians Kozelski and Miloslowsky especially helped to form his taste, and he soon became a critic well known in the galleries. It was the habit of Russian audiences to express their ideas and impressions on the spot. The galleries were divided into parties, with opposing artistic principles. One party hissed while the other applauded, and then and there they held debates, between the acts and even during performance. Adler soon became one of the fiercest leaders of such a party that Odessa had ever known. He stood for realism, for the direct expression of the life of the people. All else he hissed down, and did it so effectively that the actors tried to conciliate him. One season two actresses of talent, but of different schools, were playing in Odessa— Glebowa, whom Adler supported because of her naturalness, and Kozlowski, whose style was affected and artificial from Adler's point of view. After the strife between the rival parties had waged for some time very fiercely, one night Kozlowski sent for Adler, and asked him what she could do to get the great critic to join her party. Adler replied that so long as Glebowa played with such wonderful naturalness he should remain faithful to her colors, and advised Kozlowski, who was a kind of Russian Bernhardt, to change her style.

Adler's lack of education always weighed on his spirit, and his high ideals of the stage seemed to shut that art away from him. Yet his friends who heard him recite the speeches of his favorites, which he easily remembered, told him he had talent. "I wanted to believe them," Adler said, "but I always thought that the actor ought to know everything in order to interpret humanity."

But just about that time, when Adler was twenty-three years old, he heard that a theater had been started in Rumania by a Russian Jew named Gold-faden and that the actors spoke Yiddish.

"I was astonished," he said. "How could they act a play in a language without literature, in the jargon of our race, and who could be the actors?"

Soon Adler heard that the Jewish singers of hymns, who sometimes visited Odessa, and who moved him so because "they sang so pitifully," were the actors of the first Yiddish company, and his astonishment grew. In 1879, Goldfaden went to Odessa with his company, and his theater was crowded with Gentiles as well as Jews; and Adler saw with his eyes what he had hardly believed pos-sible—a Jewish company in a Yiddish play. The plays, however, seemed to Adler very poor—mainly light opera with vaudeville accompaniment—and the acting was also poor. But Israel Rosenberg, whom Adler describes as a long-faced Jew with pro-truding teeth, enormous eyes, and a mouth as wide as a saucer, amused Adler with the wit which he interpolated as he acted. Rosenberg, "more ignorant than I," says Adler, "was yet very successful." The two became intimate, and Rosenberg and Fräulein Oberländer urged Adler to go on the stage—Rosenberg because Adler at that time was comparatively rich, and the fräulein because she loved (and afterward married) the vigorous young man from Odessa. And Adler felt his education to be superior to that of these successful actors, and decided to make the experiment. To choose the stage, however, was to choose poverty, as he had begun to succeed in business, but he did not hesitate and, leaving his friends and family, he went on a tour with the company.

In the first performance he was so frightened that he did not hear his own words. He lost all his critical faculty, and played merely instinctively. It was a long time before he acted better than the average, which was at that time very low; but, finally, in a small town named Elizabetgrad, Adler learned his lesson. A critic visited the theater every night, and wrote long articles upon it, but Adler never found his name mentioned therein. He used to get up in the morning very early, before any one else, to buy the newspaper, but was always chagrined to find that the great man had overlooked him. At first he thought that the critic must have a personal spite against him, then that he was not noticed because he had only small roles. At last he was cast for a very long and emotional role. He thought that this part would surely fetch the critic, and the next morning eagerly bought a paper, but there was no criticism of the play at all. Rosenberg went to the critic and asked the reason.

"Adler spoiled the whole thing," was the reply. "His acting was unnatural and loud. I advise him to leave the stage."

"Then," said Adler, "I began to think. I cut my hair, which I had allowed to grow long after the fashion of actors, and was at first much discouraged. But thereafter I studied every role with great care, and read the classic plays, and never played a part until I understood it. Before that it was play with me; but after that it was serious work."

For a number of years Adler continued to act in the cities of Russia, and became the head of a company. In 1883, when Russia was closed to the Jewish stage, Adler took his company to London, where he nearly starved. There was no ghetto there, and the company gave occasional performances at various Yiddish clubs scattered through the city. Adler lost all his money and got into debt. His wife and child died, and at one time in despair he thought of leaving the stage. But it was too late to go back to Odessa, for he had once and for all cut himself off from his family and friends. He was falsely informed by a Jew who had been to America that to succeed there he would have to sing, dance, and speak German. So he stayed some time longer in London. The Rothschilds, Dr. Felix Adler, and others, took an interest in him, and told him that as the Jewish theater could have no future, since Yiddish must ultimately be forgotten, he had better give it up.

It was in 1887 that Adler came to New York,

where he found two Yiddish companies already well started. To avoid conflict with them, he went to Chicago, where, however, a Yiddish theater could get no foothold. Some rich Chicago people tried to induce Adler to learn English and go on the American stage; but Adler, always distrustful of his education and ability to learn, declined their offers, now much to his regret. He returned to New York, where Mogalesco and Kessler urged him to stay, but the ghetto actors in general were hostile to him, and he went back to London. The next year, however, he was visited by four of the managers of the New York ghetto companies (among them Mogalesco), vying with one another to secure Adler, whose reputation in the Jewish community was rapidly growing. He went back to New York in 1889, where he appeared first at the Germania Theater. He was advertised in advance as a Salvini, a Barrett, a Booth, as all stars combined. When he found how extravagantly he had been announced, he was angry, and wanted to go back to London, feeling that it was impossible to live up to what his foolish managers had led the people to expect. He consented to stay but refused to appear in *Uriel Acosta*, for which he was billed, preferring to begin in comedy, in order not to appear to compete with the reputation of Salvini. The play, which was called *The Ragpicker*, can still be seen in the ghetto. In it Adler tried to score as a character actor. But the people, expecting a tragedy, took *The Ragpicker* seriously, and did not laugh at all. The play fell flat, and the managers rushed before the curtain and told the audience that Adler was a poor actor, and that they had been deceived in him. Through the influence of the management, the whole company treated him with coldness and contempt, except the wife of one of the directors. She is now Mrs. Adler, and is one of the capable serious actresses at present at the People's Theater. Finally, the lease of the theater passed into Adler's hands, and he dismissed the whole company and formed a new one. Soon after began the struggle which brought about the latest development of the Yiddish stage.

For some time Adler was successful, but he grew more and more dissatisfied with his repertory. He could find no plays which seriously portrayed the life of the people or contained any serious ideas. Only the translated plays were good from his point of view; he wished something original, and looked about for a playwright. One night in a restaurant he was introduced to Jacob Gordin, who afterward wrote the greater part of the only serious original Yiddish plays which exist.

Gordin at that time had written no plays, but he was a man of varied literary activity, of a rarely good education, a thorough Russian schooling, and of uncommon intelligence and strength of character. He is Russian in appearance, a large broad-headed man with thick black hair and beard. As he told me, in his little home in Brooklyn, the history of his life, he omitted all picturesque details, and emphasized only his intellectual development. He was born in the same town as Gogol—Ubigovrod, in southern Russia —of rich parents. As a boy he frequented the theater, and like Adler, became a local critic and hissed down

what he did not approve. Like Adler, too, he was often carried off to the police station and fined. He
married early, became a schoolteacher and then a
journalist (in Russian), writing every sort of article,
except political, and often sketches and short stories
for newspapers and periodicals in Odessa, where he
finally controlled a newspaper—the *Odessakiano-
vosti*. He was a great admirer of Tolstoy, and desiring to live on a farm to put into practice Tolstoy's
ideas, he came to America in 1891, and nearly
starved. He became an editor of a Russian newspaper
in New York and contributed to other journals. In his
own paper he wrote violent articles against the Russian government as well as literary sketches. In Russia, Gordin had never been in a Yiddish theater, and
when he met Adler in the New York restaurant he
knew little of the conventional Yiddish play. So he
wrote his first play in a fresh spirit, with only the
character of the people and his own ideals to work
from. *Siberia*, produced in 1892, was a success with
the critics and actors, and may fairly be called the
first original Yiddish play of the better type.

The play struck a new note. It fell into line with
the Russian spirit of realism now so marked in intellectual circles in the ghetto. Life and types are what
Gordin tried for, and Jacob Adler had found his playwright. Since then Gordin has written about fifty
plays, some of which have been successful, and
many have been marked by literary and dramatic
power. Some of the better ones are *Siberia*, *The Jewish King Lear*, *The Wild Man*, *The Jewish Priest*, *Solomon Kaus*, *The Slaughter*, and *The Jewish Queen*

*Madam Liptzen*

*Lear.* Jacob Adler has been until recently his chief interpreter, although Mogalesco, Kessler, and Thomashevsky take his plays.

For several years an actress, Mrs. Liptzen, was the main interpreter of Gordin's plays. She is one of the most individual, if not one of the most skillful, actresses on the stage of New York's ghetto, and is sometimes spoken of in the quarter as the Yiddish Duse. She is the only actress of the East Side who is thus compared, by a subtitle, with a famous Gentile artist, although in many directions there is a great tendency in the ghetto to adopt foreign names and ideas. As a matter of fact, her art is exceedingly limited, but she has the unusual distinction of appearing only in the best plays, steadfastly refusing to take part in performances which she deems to be dramatically unworthy. She consequently appears very seldom, usually only in connection with the production of a new play by Jacob Gordin, who at present writes many of his plays with the Yiddish Duse in mind.

Mrs. Liptzen was born in Zhitomir, South Russia, and was interested exclusively in the stage from her childhood. The founder of the Yiddish stage, Abraham Goldfaden, and Jacob Adler played in her town for a few nights when she was about eighteen years old. Her parents were Orthodox Jews, and to go to the theater she was forced to resort to subterfuge. She became acquainted with Goldfaden and Adler, and ran away from home in order to accompany them as an actress. At first she sang and acted in such popular operatic plays as *Der Shmendrik,* and continued for three years in Russia, until the Yiddish theater was forbidden there. Then she went with a new company to Berlin, where the whole aggregation nearly starved. They were reduced to selling all their stage properties, the proceeds of which were made away with by a dishonest agent. During the time their performances in Berlin continued, Mrs. Liptzen received, it is said, the sum of ten pfennigs (two and one-half cents) a day, on which she lived. She paid five pfennigs for lodging and five pfennigs for bread and coffee, and there is left in her now a correspondingly amazing impression of the cheapness with which she could live in Germany in those days.

Jacob Adler was at that time in London with a company, eking out a miserable existence. He wrote to Mrs. Liptzen's husband, an invalid in Odessa, to send his wife to London to play in his company. About 1886 Mrs. Liptzen went to London and played in *Esther von Engedi* (the Jewish *Othello*), *Leah the Forsaken, Rachel, The Jews*, etc. In London she stayed three years, when, the theater having burned down, she went with Adler to Chicago. They tried to find a place in New York, but the Yiddish company already in New York, with Kessler and Mogalesco at its head, froze them out, and they tried to get a foothold in Chicago. A little later Mrs. Liptzen left Chicago for New York, called by the Yiddish company there to play leading parts. She began in New York with *Leah the Forsaken*, and received only ten dollars for the first three performances. It is said that she now receives from one to two hundred dollars for every performance, a fact indicating not only her growth in popularity but also the great financial success of the Yiddish theaters in New York.

Twelve years ago Mrs. Liptzen retired for a time from the stage, the reason being that there were no new plays in which she desired to appear, since the demand was entirely supplied by the romantic and historical operatic playwrights, Professor Horowitz and Mr. Latteiner.

It was not until Jacob Gordin came into prominence as a realistic playwright that Mrs. Liptzen came out of her dignified retirement. Jacob Adler was the first to play Gordin's pieces, but he played many others, too, trying in a practical way gradually to make the cause of realism triumphant. Mrs. Liptzen, however, made no compromise, and kept quiet until she was able to get the plays she wanted, which soon were written by Gordin.

Mrs. Liptzen's first success with a Gordin play was in *Medea,* for which Gordin received, it is said, the enormous sum of eighty-five dollars—having sold plays previous to that time for the well-fixed price of thirty-five dollars. *Medea's Youth,* written by Gordin for Mrs. Liptzen, was a failure, although the author thought so well of it as a literary production that he had it translated into English. The next of Mrs. Liptzen's successes was *The Jewish Queen Lear,* for which Gordin received two hundred dollars—an enormous sum for a Yiddish playwright in those days. *The Slaughter* was produced two years ago, and last year Mrs. Liptzen appeared in Gordin's *The Oath,* a Yiddish production of *Fuhrmann Henschel.* Of late Mr. Gordin's plays have been produced by a younger actress of more varied talent than Mrs. Liptzen—Mrs. Bertha Kalisch, on the whole a much worthier interpreter than the older woman.

It is Adler, however, who has been the belligerent promoter of the original and serious Yiddish drama. In 1893 he tried to introduce Gordin's plays and the new spirit of realism and literature into his company at the Windsor Theater. But the old style is still strong in popular affection, and Adler's company rebelled. Whereupon Adler went to Russia to form a new company which would be more amenable to his ideas. He came back with the new troupe, and ordered a new play from Gordin, who produced *The Jewish King Lear*. At the first reading of the play the company protested, but Adler begged for a trial, telling them that they did not know what a good play was. The play proved a great and deserved success, and is now frequently repeated. It contains several scenes of great power, and portrays with faithful art the life of the Russian Jew. In 1894 Adler tried the experiment of leasing a small theater, the Rumania, in which nothing but plays which expressed his ideas should be presented. A number of Gordin's plays were given, but the theater had much the same fate that would befall a theater uptown which played only the ideally best. It failed completely. After that, both Adler and Gordin were compelled to compromise. Adler is now associated with a company which presents every kind of play known to the ghetto, and Gordin has had to introduce horseplay and occasional vaudeville and comic opera into his plays. Even the best of the Yiddish plays contain these excrescences.

But both Adler and Gordin, while remaining practical men with an eye to the box office receipts, are working to eliminate more and more of what is distasteful to them and impertinent to art. A year ago last autumn Gordin succeeded in having his latest play, *The Slaughter*, performed without any vaudeville accompaniment. He deemed it a triumph, particularly as it was successful, and felt a debt of gratitude to Mrs. Liptzen, who produced the play without insisting on unworthy interpolations.

Gordin now hopes that the days of compromise for him are past, and Adler expects to secure some day a theater in which he can successfully produce only the serious plays of Jewish life. But both these men are pessimistic about the future of dramatic art in the ghetto. They feel not only the weight of the commercial spirit, but also the imminent death of their stage. For the Jews of the ghetto, as they become Americanized, are liable to lose their instinctive Yiddish, and then there will be no more drama in that tongue. The only Yiddish stage, worthy of the name, in the world will probably soon be no more. Jacob Adler consequently regrets that his Yiddish confines him to the Bowery stage, and Jacob Gordin longs to have his plays translated and produced on the English stage.

Mogalesco, the actor, who has, perhaps, the greatest talent of them all, whose dramatic art was born with the Yiddish stage, and who is equally happy in a *comedietta* by Latteiner or a character play by Gordin, is, like the true actor, without ideas, but always felicitous in interpretation, and enthusiastically loved by the Jewish playgoers. He and Adler, if they had been fortunate enough to have received a training consistently good, and had acted in a language of wider appeal, would easily have taken their places among those artistically honored by the world. Even as it is, they have with Gordin, with Kessler, with Mrs. Liptzen, with Mrs. Kalisch and the rest, the distinction of being prominent figures in the short career of the Yiddish stage, which, founded by Goldfaden in 1876, in Rumania, has received today, in New York, its highest and almost exclusive development.

---

In 1902 the immigrants had not yet learned about Christy Mathewson or Ty Cobb; the heroes like Theodore Roosevelt or Al Smith were still to come. So the folk heroes of the ghetto were the actors, the journalists, the cantors, the critics, the playwrights, and the composers; but mostly the actors.

The greatest of the actors were Jacob P. Adler, David Kessler, and Boris Thomashevsky. All the tales ever told, especially those describing gastronomic and sexual prowess, were retold anew with modern heroes—Adler, Kessler, and Thomashevsky. I have never yet met an East Side Jew who didn't have a favorite story about them. Although Kessler stories centered on food rather than bed, Adler and Thomashevsky were considered trenchermen, too. Thomashevsky and Adler were the Don Juans of the ghetto. Each of them traveled with a court of hangers-on, like prototypical Frank Sinatras, and spread in an East Side café, each instructed flunkies to ward off worshipers. Safe, the actor washed down the caviar and eggs and potato *latkes* with huge goblets of Rhine wine and seltzer.

So important was the Yiddish theater that when David Kessler's Second Avenue Theater opened around 1912, the preparations were carried on with the enthusiasm reserved for a world's fair. I believe the governor was there, and the mayor cut the string in front of the box office. David Kessler opened in the most famous of all East Side

dramas, *Gott, Mensch und Teufel,* a loose adaptation of
*Faust.*

One of the contributions the East Side made to the
American culture was the "theater party." Everyone has
theater parties today, from a Hempstead Hadassah to the
Vassar Alumnae Association. But the theater party was
invented by immigrant Jews around the turn of the century.

One rarely heard the statement, "I'm going to the
theater." Instead one said, "I'm going to a benefit." "Benefit" was one of the first English words the immigrants
learned, and probably one of the most important. Organizations sold theater benefit tickets to immigrants as they
came off the gangplank. All the Jewish organizations,
*vereins,* and fraternities were partly financed by benefits.

As a boy, I sat through many of them. My father was
president of the Mikulinczer *verein.* The Mikulinczers
ran a benefit five or six times a year. My father always
made a speech between the second and third acts. A
Mikulinczer benefit proceeded like the Vassar theater
party. The organization bought every seat in the house at
a discount, sold the tickets to members and friends, and
the net profit went to a predesignated cause.

This was my introduction to the theater and I shall
always be grateful for it. I thrill to this day remembering
Madame Bertha Kalisch, Kessler, and a man who would
have been a great comedian on any stage, Zelig Mogalesco.

Often the plays depicted the patterns of ghetto life
with surprising fidelity. Basically the people came to cry
at scenes which more or less depicted their own problems: the family experience with a wayward son, an un-
grateful daughter, an old-fashioned father, a cruel stepmother. Many of the immigrants had families in the old
country. The Yiddish theater helped them to remember
and to cry. A famous soprano, Lucy Gherman, made a career out of the song *"Eibiga Mama"* ("Eternal Mother"),

and thousands of shop girls wept through every performance of Jennie Goldstein, who sang *"Ich Bin ein Mama"*
("I Am a Mother").

Ocasionally Shakespeare was translated literally, but
more often only the theme was used and adapted to contemporary life. Mr. Hapgood tells of *The Jewish Hamlet*
he saw. *The Jewish King Lear* was another popular
adaptation.

Critics? There were thousands of them. Ben-Gurion
of Israel once said he was the head of a nation with one
and a half million prime ministers. By the same token,
the Yiddish stage had fifty thousand regular critics. No
one saw a show for simple enjoyment. Everybody was a
critic, reciting observations to everyone—in the shop, in
the store, in the coffee house, and in the lodge hall. Most
plays qualified only as a *shmahta* (a rag), but the word
*shmahta* is far more explosive than its literal translation.

"How did you like the show last night?" The fellow at
the workbench shrugged his shoulders and said, "A
*shmahta*." He did not know, of course, that what he had
seen the evening before was a Yiddish adaptation of Ibsen's *Doll's House*.

There were many theaters, but the benefits took place
for the most part in three: the People's Theater, the
Windsor Theater, and the Thalia. As I remember it, the
Thalia was the ritziest—no babies were allowed inside.

The actors hated the benefits as much as actors today
hate theater parties. The audience came not so much to
see the play but to see who else came. Their attention
was bad. They brought children. And they talked! Theater parties or benefits—how they talk! They talked more
than the actors.

Plays never ran long, twelve days at the most, and
more usually three or four. Sometimes families went to
the theater three times a week. In those days, prices
scaled from twenty-five cents to a dollar. It is a long way
from a Mikulinczer benefit to a Daughters of the Ameri-

can Revolution theater party, but only the prices have changed.

We have not really begun to appraise the influence of the Yiddish theater on the English-speaking stage, motion pictures, radio, and television. That crusty old Mayor Gaynor, in 1911, saw it even as it was happening: "You came to this land but yesterday and now will give us that learning and culture which has produced such players as Bonne, and Von Sonnenthal, and Rachel, and Bernhardt."

The most popular player of the era was Adler. It was my good fortune to see Mr. Adler in the old Knickerbocker Theater on Broadway at the end of his career. It was a benefit performance and every Broadway star of stage, opera, and concert world came to pay homage to the great Yiddish actor. Each insisted on "going on" in his honor, and the show lasted till five o'clock in the morning. Mr. Adler himself performed a scene from *King Lear*. I remember particularly Al Jolson singing *"Vesti la Giubba,"* followed by Giovanni Martinelli leading the audience in "Pack Up Your Troubles in Your Old Kit Bag and Smile, Smile, Smile."

Everyone who reads this and can remember the old days will want to tell a favorite anecdote about an actor. Let me, therefore, tell mine first. Adler was on tour. (In all the stories, Jacob Adler or Boris Thomashevsky was on tour.) Before his performance a handsome young woman with a four-year-old child came to the great man's dressing room. "Mr. Adler, you remember me?" she asked. "When you were here five years ago you invited me to supper after the performance?" And with this she pushed the little boy ahead of her, "And this is the result —this little boy is your own son." Adler looked at the child with real satisfaction. "That's a nice boy, a really nice boy," he said. "Here, my dear, are two tickets to tonight's performance. Take the boy, you'll both like the show." The woman began to stammer. "But Mr. Adler, this is your own son—we don't need theater tickets, our problem is to eat, we need bread." Adler shrugged and said, "You want bread, you go with a baker. From me you get tickets."

There must be many of my contemporaries who remember the famous Grossman poster announcing a new *pyessa* (a new play): "SAMUEL B. GROSSMAN, PRODUCER AND ACTOR, PRESENTS THE SORROWING FATHER, A NEW PLAY IN THREE ACTS BY SAMUEL GROSSMAN, WITH IRVING GROSSMAN, JOSEPH GROSSMAN, HELEN GROSSMAN, FANNY GROSSMAN; DANCES BY HELEN GROSSMAN; STAGE DESIGNER, MIRIAM GROSSMAN. FOR BENEFITS WRITE TO TREASURER JOSEPH GROSSMAN."

I'd like to say another word about the ghetto's tremendous interest in the theater. A few years after Mr. Hapgood wrote this book, the Neighborhood Playhouse was established on Grand Street. It was on that stage that Bernard Shaw's *Major Barbara* was produced for the first time in America. Indeed, some of the plays of Ibsen and Sudermann also made their first American appearance there.

The Neighborhood Playhouse sponsored an event which received national attention. On April 23, 1915, Ellen Terry came from England to give readings from Shakespeare. The greatest actress of the day was interested in the career of Lillian D. Wald of the Henry Street Settlement and accepted an invitation to honor Shakespeare's anniversary at the Neighborhood Playhouse in the heart of New York's Lower East Side. It was an event which filled the Jewish ghetto with a feeling of wonder and joy.

---

# six

# THE NEWSPAPERS

Yiddish newspapers have, as compared with their contemporaries in the English language, the strong interest of great freedom of expression. They are controlled rather by passion than by capital. It is their joy to pounce on controlling wealth and to take the side of the laborer against the employer. A large proportion of the articles are signed, a custom in striking contrast with that of the American newspaper. The prevalence of the unsigned article in the latter is held by the Yiddish journals to illustrate the employer's tendency to arrogate everything to himself and to make the paper a mere organ of his own policy and opinions. The remark of one of the Jewish editors, that the "Yiddish newspaper's freedom of expression is limited by the penal code alone" has its relative truth. It is, of course, equally true that the new freedom of the Jews, who in Russia had no journal in the common Yiddish, runs in these New York papers into an emotional extreme, a license which is apt to distort the news and to give over the editorial pages to virulent party disputes.

Nevertheless, the Yiddish press, particularly the socialistic branch of it, is an educative element of great value in the ghetto. It has helped essentially to extend the intellectual horizon of the Jew beyond the boundaries of the Talmud, and has largely displaced the rabbi in the position of teacher of the people. Not only do these papers constitute a forum of discussion, but they publish frequent translations of the Russian, French, and German modern classics, and for the first time lay the news of the world before the poor Jewish people. An event of moment to the Jews, such as a riot in Russia, comes to New York in private letters and is printed in the papers here often before the version "prepared" by the Russian govern-

*A newsboy*

ment appears in the Russian newspapers. Thus a Jew on the East Side received a letter from his father in Russia asking why the reserves there had been called out, and the son's reply gave him the first information about the war in China.

The make-up of the Yiddish newspaper is in a general way similar to that of its American contemporary. The former is much smaller, however, containing only about as much reading matter as would fill six or eight columns of a downtown newspaper. The sporting department is entirely lacking, the Jew being utterly indifferent to exercise of any kind. They are all afternoon newspapers and draw largely for

*A ghetto newspaper office*

the news upon the morning editions of the American papers. The staff is very limited, consisting of a few editors and, usually, only one reporter for the local news of the quarter. They give more space proportionately than any American paper to pure literature (chiefly translations, though there are some stories founded on the life of the East Side) and to scientific articles of popular character. The interesting feature of these newspapers, however, consists in their rivalries and their differences in principle. This can be presented most simply in a short sketch of their history.

## THE CONSERVATIVE JOURNALS

Yiddish journalism in New York began about thirty years ago, and continued in unimportant and unrepresentative newspapers until about twelve years ago, when the *Tageblatt,* the first daily newspaper, and the *Arbeiterzeitung* (an important socialistic weekly, now defunct but from which developed the present socialist dailies) came into existence. The *Tageblatt,* which has maintained its general character from the beginning, is the most conservative, as well as the oldest, of the daily newspapers of the ghetto. It is national and Orthodox, and fights tooth and nail for whatever is distinctively Jewish in customs, literature, language, and religion. It hates the reform sects in religion and the socialistic tendencies in politics and economics. It is called a capitalist paper by its opponents, and is so in the sense that it is more dependent upon its advertisements than the socialistic papers, which are partly supported by frequent entertainments and balls to which all their friends go. And yet how little capitalistic is even this paper is shown by the fact that while it takes a noncommittal attitude toward strikes in the Ghetto, it supports those which occur outside.

Sympathetic with workingmen and not antagonistic to the employers of the ghetto, the *Tageblatt* conventionally unites all the Jewish interests it consistently can, and has admittedly the largest circulation of any daily paper in the ghetto. The socialists call it bourgeois as well as capitalistic (which is the most horrid of all words in the quarter). Some call it chauvinistic because of its strong nationalist tendency, and fanatic because it upholds the religion of the Jews. The Jew who wants first of all to be an American and up to date hates the *Tageblatt* as tending to strengthen the distinction between Jew and Gentile. This paper goes so far in its conservatism that, according to its enemies, it condemns all rabbis who mention the name of Christ in their sermons and holds to a strict interpretation of Talmudic Law in regard to habits of life. "It is only the old-fashioned greenhorns," said the editor of one of the other papers, "coming from the old country, who will stand for it."

## THE SOCIALIST PAPERS

The socialist weekly, the *Arbeiterzeitung*, marked the beginning of the most vital journalism of the East

Side, and stood in striking contrast to the *Tageblatt*. In the circumstances attending its development into the two existing rival socialistic papers, the *Vorwärts* and the *Abendblatt*, a picture of the progressive and passionate character of the Russian-Jewish socialists of the ghetto is presented, and some of the most important and picturesque personages. The most educated and intelligent among the Jews of the East Side speak Russian, and are reactionary in politics and religion. Coming from Russia as they do, they have a fierce hatred of government and capitalism, and a

*In the office of the* Vorwärts

more or less Tolstoyan love for the peasant and the workingman. The purpose of the organizers of the *Arbeiterzeitung* publishing association was to educate the people, promulgate the doctrines of socialism, and be altogether the organ of the workman against the employer. From the outset, beginning in 1890, the *Arbeiterzeitung* was a popular and influential paper.

All the older journals had affected a Germanized Yiddish, which the people did not understand, but the new paper, aiming at the modern heart of the ghetto, carried on its propaganda in the pure Yiddish and, growing enormously in circulation, forced the language down the throats of the conservative journals. In this popular tongue, the *Arbeiterzeitung* carried on for five years a most energetic campaign for a broad socialism, admitting all allied movements in favor of common ownership, directing and encouraging strikes, printing popular scientific articles, realistic stories, dramatic criticisms, and expressing and leading generally the best intelligence of the Yiddish community. With the constituency of which this journal was the organ, socialism had almost the force and passion of a religious movement. An example of the paper's power was in connection with the Bakers' Union. That organization imposed a label on all bread made in the ghetto, and insisted that all the bakers should handle only bread of that brand. The *Arbeiterzeitung* supported the union so effectively that no other bread could possibly be obtained in the quarter. At the first *Yahresfest* of the journal, Cooper Union overflowed with enthusiastic workingmen, and long lines of the excluded stretched out down the Bowery to Houston Street.

The man whose name is most intimately connected with the *Arbeiterzeitung* is its former editor, Abraham Cahan, now known outside of the ghetto as a writer in English of novels and short stories of Jewish life. He is of the best type of the ethical agitator. A convincing and impassioned speaker, he has held hundreds of workingmen by his clear and strongly expressed ideas, whether written in his paper or spoken at nightly meetings in some poor hall on the East Side, where the men gathered after the labors of the day. Twice he went abroad to speak at international labor conferences. At the same time that he supported the definite cause of the Social Democratic party, he put the same energy and passion into the education of the people in scientific and literary directions. He spoke and wrote for directness, simplicity, and humanity. In art, therefore, the realistic school of Russian writers, of whom in our generation there have been so many great men, received his fighting allegiance. For five years Cahan put all his intelligence and devotion into this work, and the power of the *Arbeiterzeitung* was partly his power. Today in the ghetto, where fierce jealousies are rampant, Cahan is admitted to be the man, among many men of energy, intelligence, and devotion, who has wielded most influence in the community.

A literary and dramatic event happened in 1892 which showed the power of Cahan and his socialist associates in influencing the taste of the ghetto. It was the production of Gordin's drama *Siberia*. Up to that time, nothing but conventional opera, melo-drama, and historical plays had been given on the Bowery, but the day after the performance of *Siberia,* the *Arbeiterzeitung* contained Cahan's long review of the play, welcoming it enthusiastically as an event breaking the way for realistic art in the colony. Since then this type of play has taken a prominent place in the repertory at the Yiddish theaters. For five years the *Arbeiterzeitung* continued its influence, but then came a split among the socialists, which resulted in two daily papers—the *Abendblatt* and the *Vorwärts.*

Cahan, Miller, and others of the men who had started the *Arbeiterzeitung* gradually lost control through the share system which had been inaugu-rated. They desired to maintain a liberal policy to-ward all labor movements and to allow the literary and socialistic societies to be represented in the pa-per, but the other faction wanted the newspaper to be exclusively an organ of socialism in its narrow sense. The result was that soon after the publication of the *Arbeiterzeitung* as the daily *Abendblatt,* Cahan re-signed the editorship and turned, disgusted, to Eng-lish newspapers and to realistic fiction, in which he was absorbed until recently. A few months ago he re-sumed the editorship of the *Vorwärts* after an absence of several years from participation in Yiddish jour-nalism. Louis Miller, a witty and energetic socialist and writer, who had from the first been active in the management of the *Arbeiterzeitung,* was one of the most prominent of the men who continued the fight against the narrower socialistic element—a fight which resulted in the establishment in 1897 of the other socialist daily now existing, the *Vorwärts*.

---

I sold newspapers in the ghetto of New York between the years 1911 and 1917. I sold the newspapers after school and on Sunday mornings, and of course, during the summer vacation. I shouted *"Vorwärts! Varheit! Tageblatt! Tog!"*. These were the important evening papers in those days. Before America got into the war in 1917, we newsboys learned a trick about shouting the "Extras." The East Side Jews were overwhelmingly pro-German. Most of them had felt the cruelty of czarist oppression. While the immigrants made fun of the "fancy" German Jews, they had a healthy respect for Germany and its culture. The Jews of the East Side wanted to see Russia humbled. So we newsboys shouted "extra" whenever there was a Russian defeat, but more often we exaggerated to turn every skirmish into shouts in Yiddish of: "Extra! Extra! Russians Retreat Again!"

One of the proud episodes in the history of American journalism was the rise of the Yiddish press in the ghetto of New York. The first daily was the *Tageblatt* ("Jewish Daily News"), which was founded in 1885; a later daily, established in 1891, was the *Teglicher Herold* ("Daily Herald"), which was merged into the *Varheit* ("Truth") and was later absorbed by the *Tog* ("The Day"). A third daily was the *Vorwärts* ("Forward"), a liberal trade-union paper that eventually was to achieve the largest circulation of any foreign-language publication in the English-speaking world.

Also of importance was the *Jewish Morning Journal*, established in 1901 as the spokesman of the Orthodox and non-radical community. For many years the *Jewish Morning Journal* supported most of the national and statewide Republican candidates.

In 1928, the *Jewish Morning Journal* was merged with the *Tageblatt* and eventually consolidated with the *Tog*. (The *Tog-Jewish Morning Journal*, and the *Vorwärts* were still publishing in 1964.)

In addition to these daily newspapers there were literally dozens of weeklies, monthlies, quarterlies, and annuals, some devoted to literature and humor, others published by political parties, labor unions, *Landsmanschaften*, Zionist organizations, and cultural and professional groups.

The labor organizations and the radical movements began to edge out the importance of the synagogue. So, too, socially, did the lodges and societies. The Yiddish press, the stage, and the lecture platform became the great influences on life in the ghetto.

Created by and for immigrants, the Yiddish press flourished as long as mass immigration continued. It represents one of the great stories in the history of American journalism. This Yiddish press taught the immigrants about America, kept them in touch with the happenings in the Old World, and promoted political culture and social integration.

The dominant figure in Jewish journalism was Abraham Cahan, who from 1902 to 1951, was editor of the *Vorwärts*. Mr. Cahan was a successful writer in English, having contributed to several national magazines, before he took his place in Jewish journalism and became, for at least a million men, women, and children, the mediator between the Yiddish and American cultures. Mr. Cahan built the *Vorwärts* from a circulation of five thousand to a modern newspaper that reached a daily circulation of over a quarter of a million in its heyday.

The *Vorwärts* carried much human-interest material. Mr. Cahan once wrote a story about an Italian barber who had fallen in love with a Jewish girl on Broome Street. The barber wanted to marry her, but her mother wouldn't hear of it. Finally the mother said that they could be married if the barber converted to Judaism. She made him learn Hebrew and pray every morning with a *yarmulke* over his head. The couple lived with the mother-in-law, and the barber couldn't get his breakfast until he prayed. But that wasn't all. The girl had a brother named Joe, and Joe didn't pray before breakfast. After a while, the barber asked his mother-in-law, "Why doesn't Joe have to pray before breakfast?" The answer was: "He's a Jew. I *know* he's a Jew. *You've* got to prove it."

One of the most interesting features of the *Vorwärts* was the *Bintel Brief*—letters to the editor. Here are a few of them as edited by George M. D. Wolfe. These letters were written between 1906 and 1908 and Mr. Wolfe translated them in a study of social philosophy at the Training School for Jewish Social Work:

*"My little girl wants to pierce her ears for earrings. She says all the girls here have pierced ears, but my husband says no, that in America you do not pierce ears any more, but the girl is crying, and tell my husband in the letter what is the best to do."*

*"My son was against my marriage, but I have left my second husband and I am getting a divorce. My son reads the Vorwärts, and I plead with him to forgive me. I am lonely as a stone."*

*"My husband reads the Vorwärts, but where does he read it? In the barbershop where he goes all the time with those other card players. Let him see this letter."*

*"Is it a sin to use face powder? Shouldn't a girl look beautiful? My father does not want me to wear face powder. Is it a sin?"*

*"My son is already twenty-six years old and he doesn't want to get married. He says he is a socialist and he is too*

*busy. Socialism is socialism and getting married is impor-*
*tant, too."*

"I am a socialist and going with an American girl. She
wants to go to dances and to balls and to affairs, and I
would like to know whether you think it is all right for
me to go too."

"I am a socialist and my boss is a fine man. I know he's
a capitalist, but I cannot hate him. Am I doing the wrong
thing?"

Abe Cahan was among the first political journalists
in America to recognize that communism was a threat
to democratic institutions. He saw this even before the
Bolshevik revolution and remained consistent in his op-
position for the rest of his life. In the early 1930's, he
secured credentials from Senator William Borah to send
his Sunday editor, Harry Lang, on a trip to Russia.
When Lang began his series of articles on the totalitar-
ianism of the Soviet Union, and the articles were translated in the New York *Evening Journal,* many uptown
conservatives called these old social-democrats "red-
baiters," and the communists burned Cahan and Lang
in effigy in Union Square.

---

These two socialist dailies—the *Vorwärts* and the
*Abendblatt*—were (until recently, when the *Abendblatt* died) bitter rivals. The *Abendblatt* was devoted
to the interests of the Socialist Labor party while the
*Vorwärts* supports in a general way the Social Democratic party, although it is not so distinctively a party
paper as was the *Abendblatt*. The adherents of the
latter paper looked upon the *Vorwärts* as unreliable,
and the *Vorwärts* people thought the *Abendblatt* intolerant. The *Abendblatt* prided itself on its uncom-
promising character, and the *Vorwärts* is content to

adapt itself to what it deems the present needs of the Jewish community. Thus the *Vorwärts* is willing to join hands with reform movements in general, with trades unions, etc., while the *Abendblatt* stiffly demanded that allied organizations should enter the socialist camp. The triumph of the *Vorwärts* was therefore a triumph of the more liberal spirits.

Two other daily publications are more distinctively mere newspapers than the two socialistic organs, and make no consistent attempt to influence public opinion, at least in the definite direction of a movement. The *Abend-Post* seems to have no very distinctive policy or character; it is neither socialistic nor conservative Jewish. The distinction it aims at is to be a newspaper simply, to reflect events and not to determine opinion. In the editor's words, the *Abend-Post* "is not chauvinistic, like the *Tageblatt;* the Jew does not resound in it. It aims to Americanize the ghetto, and diminish or ignore the chasm between Jew and Gentile." The editor of one of the socialist papers calls this sort of thing by another name. "The *Abend-Post,*" he said, " is an imitation of American yellow journalism." A fifth daily, the *Herald*, is even less distinctive than the *Abend-Post*. It has no party and is not as sensational as the other. It might, perhaps, be called the Jewish mugwump.

Recently another daily, the *Jewish World*, has been organized under favorable auspices. Its avowed policy is to bridge the chasm which exists between sons and fathers in the ghetto, to make the sons more Hebraic and the fathers more American, the sons more conservative and the fathers more progressive.

Connected with its management is H. Masliansky, one of the most impassioned orators of the ghetto.

The question of the circulation figures of these five important dailies (the conservative *Tageblatt,* the *Abend-Post,* the *Herald,* the *Vorwärts,* and the now-defunct *Abendblatt*) is a difficult one. About the only thing that seems certain is that the *Tageblatt* leads in this respect. Even the editors of the other papers admit that, although they differ as to the absolute figures. The editor of the *Tageblatt* places his paper's circulation at forty thousand, the *Abend-Post* at fourteen thousand, the *Herald* next, and the two socialistic papers last, which ending is a felicitous consummation for the editor of the most conservative newspaper in the ghetto. The editor of the *Abend-Post* says the *Tageblatt* leads with a daily issue of about thirty thousand, the *Abend-Post* coming next with twenty-three thousand seven hundred, the *Herald* and the socialist papers stringing out in the rear. The editors of the socialist sheets naturally give a somewhat different order. Mr. Miller of the *Vorwärts* puts the actual circulation of the *Tageblatt* at about seventeen thousand; his own paper, the *Vorwärts,* next, with about fourteen thousand daily except on Saturday (the Jewish Sunday) when the number ranges between twenty and twenty-five thousand, owing to the fact that the conservative newspapers (*i.e.,* those that are not socialistic) do not appear on that day. The circulation of the rival socialistic paper, the *Abendblatt,* he puts at about eight thousand. In these figures there is no attempt at entire accuracy.

There are several Yiddish weekly and monthly journals published in New York. The *Tageblatt*, *Abend-Post*, and *Herald* have weekly editions, but by far the most interesting of the papers which are not dailies are the two anarchistic sheets, the *Freie Arbeiterstimme*, a weekly, and the *Freie Gesellschaft*, a monthly.

Contrary to the general impression of the character of these people, in which bombs play a large part, the anarchists of the ghetto are a gentle and idealistic body of men. The abnormal activity of the Russian Jews is this country is expressed by the socialists rather than the anarchists. The latter are largely theorists and aim rather at the education of the people by a journalistic exploitation of their general principles than by a warlike attitude toward specific events of the time. Their attitude is not so partisan as that of the socialists. They quarrel less among themselves, and are characterized by dreamy eyes and an unpractical scheme of things. They believe in nonresistance and the power of abstract right, and are trying to work out a peaceful revolution, maintaining that the violence often accompanying the movement in Europe is due to the fact that many anarchists are passionate individuals who in their indignation do not live up to their essentially gentle principles. The socialists aim at a more strictly centralized government even than any one existing, since they desire the whole machinery of production and distribution to be in the hands of the community. The anarchists

S. Janowsky

desire no government whatever, believing that law works against the native dignity of the individual, and they trust to man's natural goodness to maintain order under free conditions. A man's own conscience only can punish him sufficiently, they think. The socialists go in vividly for politics, while the anarchists have nothing to do with them. The point on which these two parties agree is the common hatred of private property.

The weekly anarchistic paper, the *Freie Arbeiterstimme*, prints about seven thousand copies. Out of this circulation, with the assistance of balls, entertainments, and benefits at the theaters, the paper is able to exist. It pays a salary to only one man, the editor, S. Janowsky, who receives the sum of thirteen dollars a week. He is a little dark-haired man, with beautiful eyes, and soft, persuasive voice. He thinks that government is so corrupt that the anarchists need do little to achieve their ends, that silent forces are at work which will bring about the great day of anarchistic communism. In his newspaper he tries to educate the common people in the principles of anarchy. The aim is popular, and the more intelligent exploitation of the cause is left to the monthly *Freie Gesellschaft*, which with the same principles as the *Freie Arbeiter-stimme*, has a higher literary and philosophical character. The editors and contributors are men of culture and education, and work without any pay. It is still gentler and more pacific in its character than the weekly *Freie Arbeiter-stimme*, of whose comparatively contemporaneous and agitatory method it disapproves calmly; believing, as the editors of the monthly do, that a weekly paper cannot exist without giving the people something other than the ideally best. With reference to the ideally best, a number of serious, contemplative men gather in a basement opposite the Hebrew Institute, the headquarters of the *Freie Gesellschaft*, and there talk about the subjects often discussed within its pages, such as Slavery and Freedom, Darwinism and Communism, Man and Government, the Purpose of Education, etc.,—any broad economic subject admitting of abstract treatment.

The talk of these anarchists is distinguished by a high idealism and an unpractical and devoted attitude. One of the foremost among them (they say they have no leaders, as that would be against individual liberty) is Katz, literary editor of the *Vorwärts*, a contributor to the anarchistic monthly, a former editor of the anarchistic weekly, and a recently successful playwright in the ghetto. His play, *The Jewish Don Quixote*, was produced at the Thalia Theater on the Bowery. Not since Gordin's *Siberia* has a play aroused such intelligent interest. The hero is a quixotic Jew, full of kindness, devotion, and love for his race and for humankind.

## SOME PICTURESQUE CONTRIBUTORS

There are many other picturesque and interesting men connected with these Yiddish journals, either as

*Katz*

A. Frumkin

editors or contributors. Morris Rosenfeld, the sweatshop poet, writes articles and occasionally poems for
the socialistic papers. Abraham Wald, the vigorous
and stormy young poet, contributes literary and socialistic articles three times a week to *Vorwärts*.
The editor of one of the conservative papers, distinguished for his logic and his clever business management, is interesting because of the facility with which
he adapts his principles to the commercial needs of
the moment. At one time he was a socialist, then became a Christian, then a Jew again simply, and now
is a conservative Jew. Another editor remarked that
he was a man of sense and logic. One of the Jews who
writes for the ghetto papers is A. Frumkin, who has
the rare distinction of having been born and educated

in Jerusalem. There he lived until he was eighteen, when he went to Constantinople and studied Turkish law. Afterward he journeyed to Paris, where he married, and then to New York, where he writes many articles in Yiddish about Jerusalem and Palestine, which are published largely in the *Vorwärts*. He is a young man of about thirty, with a fresh, rosy look and a buoyant manner. He is an anarchist, and his energetic bearing is in strong contrast to the pale cast of thought that marks his fellows, the intellectuals among the anarchists of New York. Other occasional or constant writers are the Hebrew poet Dolitzki and the poets Morris Winchevsky and Abraham Sharkansky.

These two men—Morris Winchevsky and Abraham Sharkansky—are in a class quite different from that to which Rosenfeld, Zunser, Dolitzki, and Wald belong; as opposed to the latter they are interesting rather for form than for substance. They are men with some lyric gift and a talent for verse, but are strong neither in thought nor feeling. Winchevsky is a socialist, a man who has edited more than one Yiddish publication with success, of uncommon learning and cultivation. In literary attempt he is more nearly like the ordinary American or English writer than the Jewish. Most of the ghetto poets portray the dark and sordid aspect of their lives. Most of them do it with unhappy strength; certainly one of them, Rosenfeld, does it with genius. But Winchevsky attempts to give a bright picture of things. He tries to be entertaining and heartfelt, sentimental and sweet. Truth is not so much what he attains as a little vein of sentimental verse which is sometimes touched with a true lyric quality.

Sharkansky can not be put in any intellectual category. He is a man of considerable poetic talent, but he seems to have little feeling and fewer ideas. There is no movement or tendency for which he cares. In character he is a businessman, with a detached talent unrelated to the remainder of his personality.

Philip Kranz and A. Feigenbaum, editors and writers of political editorials, are two of the most prominent men connected with the history of Yiddish journalism. They are men of energy and force and represent a large class of Jews interested in social science and political economy. A. Tannenbaum occupies a peculiar and interesting position as a writer for the newspapers. He writes very long novels, the plots of which are drawn from books in French, German, or Russian. About these plots he weaves incidents and characters from American history, and inserts popular ideas of science and philosophy. His aim is to educate the ghetto by dishing up science and philosophy in a palatable form. D. Hermalin's distinctive character is that of a translator of foreign books into Yiddish. Swift, Tolstoy, De Maupassant, have been in part translated by him into the ghetto's dialect. He, like some of the other men best known for more unpretentious work, is an author of very poor plays. David Pinsky, a writer for the *Abendblatt*, is very interesting not only as a writer of short sketches of literary value, but also as a dramatic critic and as one of the more wide-awake and distinctively modern of the young men of Yiddish

New York. He is so keen with the times that he looks even on realism with distrust. Even Silverstein, the great philosopher, the second Spinoza, a man highly respected in a professional way by eminent scientists of the day, is an occasional contributor to these interesting newspapers.

# seven

# THE SKETCH WRITERS

The Russian Jews of the East Side of New York are, in proportion as they are educated, as I have said, realists in literary faith. Is it natural? Is it true to life? they are inclined to ask of every piece of writing that comes under their eyes. As their lives are circumscribed and more or less unfortunate, their ideas of what constitutes the truth are limited and gloomy. Their criteria of art are formed on the basis of the narrow but intense work of modern Russian fiction. They look up to Tolstoy and Chekhov, and reject all principles founded upon more romantic and more genial models. The simplicity of their critical ideals lends, however, to their intellectual lives a certainty which is striking enough when compared with the varied, wavering, ungrounded literary norms and judgments of the ordinary intelligent Anglo-Saxon. The lack of authoritative literary criticism in America is partly due to the multiplicity of our classic models. With a simpler literature in mind the Russian is more constantly able to apply a decisive test.

The Russian Jew of culture when he comes to New York carries with him Russian ideals of literature. The best Yiddish work produced in America is Russian in principle. Many of the writers who publish literary sketches in the newspapers of the ghetto have written originally in the Russian language and know the Russian-Jewish life better than the life of the Yiddish East Side; and even now they write mainly about conditions in Russia. Moreover, those who know their New York and its special Jewish life thoroughly and mirror it in their work are in method, though not in material, Russian; they are close, faithful, unhappy realists.

Whatever its form, however, a considerable body of fiction is published more or less regularly in the daily and weekly periodicals of the quarter which represents faithfully the life of the poor Russian Jew in the great American city. A Gentile who knew nothing of the New York ghetto, but could read Yiddish, might get a good picture of something more than the superficial aspects of the quarter through the sketches of half a dozen of the more talented men who write for the socialist newspapers. The conditions under which the children of Israel live in New York, their manners, problems, and ideals, appear, if not with completeness, at least with suggestiveness, in these short articles, usually in fiction form, the best of them direct, simple and unpretentious, true of life in general and to the life of the Russian Jew in America in particular. The sad aspect of life predominates, but not through conventional sentimentality on the part of the writers, who are not aware that they are objects of possible pity. They merely tell without comment the facts they know. For the most part, those facts are gloomy and sordid, often lightened, however, by the sense of the ridiculous which seldom entirely deserts the Jew, and as likely as not rendered attractive by feeling and by beauty of characterization.

## SOME REALISTS

S. Libin holds the place among prose writers that Morris Rosenfeld does among poets. Like Rosenfeld, he has been a sweatshop worker, and, like him, writes about the sordid conditions of the life. The shop, the push-cart peddler, and the tenement house mark the range of his subjects; but into these unsightly things he puts constant feeling and an unfailing pathos and humor. As in the case of Rosenfeld, there are tears in everything he writes, but, unlike

*S. Libin*

Rosenfeld, he also smiles. He is a dark, thin, little man, as ragged as a tramp, with plaintive eyes and a deprecatory smile when he speaks. He is uncommonly poor, and at present sells newspapers for a living and writes an occasional sketch, for which he is paid at the rate of a dollar and a half or two dollars a column by the Yiddish newspapers. He is able to produce these little articles only on impulse and, consequently, although he is one of the more prolific of the sketch writers of the quarter, writes for relief rather than for income. Some of his contemporaries, with greater constancy to commercial ideals, have partly given up unremunerative literature for the position of newspaper hacks, but Libin, remembering his sweatshop days, does not like a boss, and is under the constant necessity of relieving his feelings by his work.

Libin lives with his wife and child in a tenement house in Harlem, where he has continually before his eyes the home conditions which form the subject of so many of his sketches. This little man, who looks like the commonest kind of a sweatshop Jew, has the simplest and sincerest interest in domestic things. With great pride he pointed out to the visitor his one-year-old baby, who lay asleep on a miserable sofa, and talked of it and of his wife, who has also been a worker in the shops, with greater pleasure even than of his sketches, which, however, he writes with joy and solace. He wept when he spoke of his child that died, and he has written poems in prose about it which weep, too. In the story of his life which he told, a common, ignorant Jew was revealed, a thorough product of the sweatshop—a man distinguished from the proletarian crowd only by a capacity for feeling and by a genuine talent. He was born in Russia twenty-nine years ago, and came to New York when he was twenty-two years old. For four years he worked as a capmaker in shops which were then more wretched than they are now, from sixteen to seventeen hours a day. While at his task he would steal a few minutes to devote to his sketches, which he sent to the *Arbeiterzeitung*. Cahan recognized in Libin's misspelled, illiterate, almost illegible manuscript a quality which worthily ranked it with good realistic literature. Since then Libin has written extensively for the *Zukunft,* a monthly now defunct, the *Truth,* published at one time by the poet Winchevsky in Boston, and for the New York daily *Vorwärts,* to which he still contributes.

One of his sketches "The New Law" (about a column and a half long) expresses one aspect of the life led by a sweatshop family. A tailor going to the shop one morning as usual, finds the boss and the other workers in a state of excitement. They have just heard about the new law limiting the day in the shop to ten hours and forbidding the men to do any work at home. This to them is a serious proposition, for, as they are paid by the piece, they need many hours to make enough to pay their expenses. The tailor goes home earlier than usual that night, about ten o'clock, with the customary bundle of clothes, for his wife and children to work over. He is tired, distressed, and irritated at the thought of the law. He finds his wife and ten-year-old daughter half-asleep as usual, but yet sewing busily. They, too, are pale and tired, and near them on the lounge is a sleeping baby, on the floor another. The little girl tries to hide her drowsiness from her father, and works more busily than ever.

"Why are you back so early?" asks his wife.

"Pretty soon," he replies morosely, "I'll be back still earlier."

"Is work slack again?" she asks, her cheek growing paler.

"It's another trouble, not that," he says. "It's a new law, a bitter law." To his little daughter he adds, "Sleep, child, you will soon have time to sleep all day."

*"New Law"*

His ignorant wife does not understand.

"A new law? What is that? What does it mean?" she asks.

"It means that I can work only ten hours a day."

Then they calculate how much money he can make in ten hours. Now he works nineteen hours, and they have nothing to spare. Under the new law he will be idle seven or eight hours a day. What will they do? She thinks the boss must be responsible for the terrible arrangement, for does not all trouble come from the boss? He is irritated by her simplicity, and she begins to weep. The little girl is overjoyed at the thought that she will no longer have to work, but tries to conceal her pleasure. The laborer, moved by his wife's tears, endeavors to comfort her.

"Ah," he says, "it's only a law! Two years ago there was one like it but the work went on just the same." But she continues to weep until their evening meal is ready, when the children are aroused from their sleep to obey "the supper law," Libin concludes in a spirit of tragicomedy.

"She Got Her Prize" is the title of a sketch in which unexhilarating comedy predominates. A laborer borrows some clothes to go to a party. In his absence his wife sells a number of rags to the old-clothes man, who innocently takes off her husband's only suit, carelessly put near the bundle he was to carry away. The husband does not notice the loss until the next day, when he has nothing to wear, cannot go to the shop, and so loses his job. "Betty" is the story of a girl who falls sick just before the day set for her wedding, and is taken to the hospital. The sketch pictures her in bed, reading a farewell letter from her lover, who has deserted her. "Misery" is a prose poem written by Libin when his child dies. It has no plot and is merely the outcry of a simple, wounded heart, telling of pain, longing and wonder at the sad mystery of the world. A pleasing rhythm runs through the Yiddish, and as the author read it aloud it seemed, indeed, like a "human document."

"A Child of the Ghetto," one of the longest and most detailed of all, is full of the sad, though gently satiric, quality of Libin's art. The author meets a peddler on Ludlow Street who recognizes him as the man who once saved his life by attracting to himself the snowballs of a number of urchins who had been plaguing the peddler one cold winter day. They have a chat, and the author asks the ragged pushcart man how he is getting on in the world. The peddler replies that all of his class have their troubles—the fruit quickly spoils, and the "bees" (policemen) come around regularly for some of the "honey." But he has a sorrow all to himself. His oldest son is a mathematician, and no good. When in the Jewish school in Russia the little fellow had learned to figure, and he had been figuring ever since. His father had found, much to his disappointment, that in America also the boy would have to spend some time in school. The "monkey business" of learning had ruined the child. He was bewitched by mathematics and studied all day long. Sent successively to a sweatshop, a grocery, to tend a pushcart, he proved thoroughly incapable of learning any trade, was absent-minded and constantly calculating, and always lost his job. And his

*"A Child of the Ghetto"*

old father bemoaned the misfortune all day long as he sold his bananas on Ludlow Street.

Younger than Libin, less mature and less devoted to his art, with a very limited amount of work done, simpler and more naive, if possible, than the older man, is Levin, a typesetter in the office of *Vorwärts*. His sketches are swifter and shorter than those of Libin, more effective and dramatic in form, with greater conventional relief of surprises and antitheses, but they have not so much feeling and do not manifest so high a degree of realistic art. In contrast with Libin, who aims only for the quiet picture of ordinary life, Levin seeks the poignant moment in the flow of daily events. With more of a commercial attitude toward his work, Levin is, consequently, in more comfortable circumstances. Like Libin, he has worked in the shops, is uneducated, and has married a tailor girl. Like Libin, again, he takes his subjects from the sweatshop, the tenement house, and the street. He is a handsome, ingenuous young fellow of twenty-two years. Only eight of these have been spent in America, yet in this short time he has worked himself into the life of Hester and Suffolk streets to such an extent that his short sketches give most faithful glimpses of various little points of human nature as it shapes itself on the East Side.

"Where Is She?" is a striking and typical incident in the career of a pushcart peddler. The itinerant seller of fruit is doing some hard thinking one day in Hester Street. He is worried about something, and does not display the activity necessary for a successful merchant of his class. A vivid picture of the street is given—the passers-by, the tenement houses, the heat. He knows that his business is suffering, but his thoughts dwell, in spite of himself, with his wife, who is about to be confined, perhaps that very day. Yesterday she had done the washing, but on this day, for the first time, remained in bed. But he must go to the street as usual. Otherwise his bananas would spoil. He worries, too, about the condition of his chil-

"Where Is She?"

dren, left without the care of their mother. A woman
crosses the street to inspect his bananas. Perhaps a
buyer, he thinks, and concentrates his attention. She
selects the best bananas, those that will keep the longest, and asks the price. "Two for a cent," he says.
"Too much," she replied. "I will give you two cents
for five." That is less than they cost him, and he refuses, and she goes away, and then he is sorry he had
not sold. Just then his little daughter runs hatless,
breathless up to him. "Mama," she says, and weeps.
She can say no more. He leaves her with the cart and
runs to the tenement house, finds his little boy playing on the floor, but his wife gone. He rushes dis-

tractedly out, looks up the stairs, and sees clothes hanging on a line on the roof, where he goes and finds his wife. She had left the bed in order to dry the wash of the day before and was unable to return. He carries her back to bed and returns to his pushcart.

"Put Off Again" is the story of a man and a girl who try to save enough money from their work in the sweatshop to marry. They need only a couple of hundred dollars for clothes and furniture, and have saved almost that sum when a letter comes from the girl's mother in Russia: her husband is dead after a long illness, and she needs money. The girl sends her seventy dollars, and the wedding is put off. The next time it is the girl's brother who arrives in New York and borrows fifty dollars to make a start in business. When they are again ready for the wedding and the day set, the young fellow quarrels with the sweatshop boss and is discharged. That is the evening before the day set for the wedding, and the young man calls on the girl and tells her. "We must put it off again, Jake," she says, "till you get another job." They cling to each other and are silent and sad.

A sketch so simple that it seems almost childish is called "The Bride Weeps." It is a hot evening, and the people in the quarter are all out on their stoops. There are swarms of children about, and a bride and groom are embracing each other and watching the crowd. "Poor people," says the bride reflectively, "ought not to have children." "What do you know about it?" asks the groom, rather piqued. Their pleasure is dampened, and she goes to bed and wets her pillow with tears.

"Fooled," one of the most interesting of Levin's sketches, is the tale of an umbrella peddler. It is very hot in the ghetto, and everybody is uncomfortable, but the umbrella peddler is more uncomfortable than any one else. He hates the bright sun that interferes with his business. It has not rained for weeks, and his stock in trade is all tied up in the house. He has no money, and wishes he were back in Russia, where it sometimes rains. He goes back to his apartment and sits brooding with his wife. "When are you going to buy us some candy, Papa?" ask the children. Suddenly his wife sees a cloud in the sky, and they all rush joyfully to the window. The sun disappears, and the clouds continue to gather. The wife goes out to buy some food; the children say, "Papa is going to the street now, and will bring us some candy," and the peddler unpacks his stock of umbrellas and puts on his rubber boots. But the clouds roll away, and the hated sun comes out again, and the peddler takes off his boots and puts his pack away. "Ain't you going to the street, Papa?" ask the children sorrowfully. "No," replies the peddler, "God has played a joke on me."

Libin and Levin, although they differ in the way described, are yet to be classed together in essentials. They are both simple, uneducated men who write unpretentious sketches about a life they intimately know. They picture the conditions almost naively without comment and without subtlety. Libin, in a way to draw tears, Levin with the buoyant optimism of healthy youth, notice the quiet things in the everyday life of the Yiddish quarter that are touching and effective.

Contrasting definitely with the sketches of Libin and Levin are those of Jacob Gordin, who, although he is best known in the ghetto as a playwright, has yet written voluminously for the newspapers. Unlike the other two, Gordin is a well-educated man, knowing thoroughly several languages and literatures, including Greek, Russian, and German. His greater resources of culture and his sharper natural wit have made of him by far the most practiced writer of the lot. With many literary examples before him, he knows the tricks of the trade, is skillful and effective, has a wide range of subjects and is full of ideas in the semiphilosophical sense. The innocent Libin and Levin are children in comparison, and yet their sketches show greater fidelity to the facts than do those of the talented Gordin, who is too apt to employ the ordinary literary devices wherever he can find them, caring primarily for the effect rather than for the truth, and almost always heightening the color to an unnatural and pretentious pitch. In the drama Gordin's tendency toward the sensational is more in place. He has the sense of character and theatrical circumstance, and works along the broad lines demanded by the stage; but these qualities, when transferred to stories from the life, result in what is sometimes called in the ghetto onion literature. So definitely theatrical, indeed, are many of his sketches that they are sometimes read aloud by the actors to crowded Jewish audiences. Another point that takes from Gordin's interest to us as a sketch writer is that his best stories have Russia rather than New York as a background, and that his sketches from New York life are comparatively unconvincing. He has a great contempt for America, which he satirizes in some of his sketches, particularly the political aspect, and intends someday to return to Russia, where he had a considerable career as a short-story writer in the Russian language. He is forty-nine years old, and, compared with the other men, is in comfortable circumstances, as he now makes a good income from his plays, which grow in popularity in the quarter. Before coming to America he taught school and wrote for several newspapers in Russia, where he was known as Ivan der Beissende, on account of the sharp character of his feuilletons. He came to this country in 1891, and shortly after, his first play, *Siberia*, was produced and made a great hit among the intellectuals and socialists of the quarter. He began immediately to write for the socialist newspapers, and also established a short-lived weekly periodical in the Russian language, which he wrote almost entirely himself.

"A Nipped Romance" is a story of two children who are collecting coals on a railway track. The boy of thirteen and the girl of eleven talk about their respective families, laying bare the sordidness, misery, and vice in which their young lives are encompassed. They know more than children ought to know, and insensibly develop a sentimental interest in each other, when a train comes along and kills them. "Without a Pass," sometimes recited in the theater by the actor Moshkovitch pictures with gruesome detail a girl working in the sweatshop. The brutal door-keeper refuses to let her go out for relief without a pass, and she dies of weakness, hunger, and cold. "A Tear," one of the best, is the tale of an old Jewish woman who has come to New York to visit her son. He is married to a Gentile, and the old lady is so much abused by her daughter-in-law that she goes back to Russia. The sketch represents her alone at the pier, about to embark. She sees the friends of the other passengers crowding the landing but no one is there to say good-by to her, and as the ship moves away a tear rolls down her cheek to the deck. "Who Laughs?" satirizes the Americans who laugh at Russian Jews because of their beards, dress, and accent. Another sketch denounces the new woman——she who apes American manners, lays aside her Jewish wig, becomes flippant and interested in movements. Still another is a highly colored contrast between woman's love and that of less-devoted man. A story illustrating how the author's desire to make an effect sometimes results in the ludicrous is the would-be pathetic wail of a calf which is about to be slaughtered.

## AMERICAN LIFE THROUGH RUSSIAN EYES

In connection with Gordin, two other writers of talent who work on the Yiddish newspapers may be briefly mentioned, although one of them has written as yet nothing and the other comparatively little that is based on the life of New York. They are, as is Gordin in his best sketches, Russian not only in form, but also in material. David Pinsky, who did general translating and critical work on the *Abendblatt* until a few months ago, when that newspaper died, has been in New York only a little more than a year and has written very little about the local quarter. He has not even as yet approached near enough to the New York life to realize that there are any special conditions to portray. He is the author, however, of good sketches in German and is somewhat different in the character of his inspiration from the other men. They are close adherents of the tradition of Russian realism, while he is under the influence of the more recent European faith that disclaims all schools in literature. His stories, although they remain faithful to the sad life portrayed, yet show greater sentimentality and some desire to bring forward the attractive side.

The other of these two writers, B. Gorin, knew his Russian-Jewish life so intimately before he came to New York seven years ago, that he has continued to draw from that source the material of his best stories, although he has written a good deal about Yiddish New York. His sketches have the ordinary Russian merit of fidelity in detail and unpretentiousness of style. Compared with the other writers in New York, he is more elaborate in his workmanship. More mature than Libin, he is free from Gordin's artistic insincerity. He has been the editor of several Yiddish papers in the quarter, and has contributed to nearly all of them.

Of Gorin's stories which touch the Russian-Jewish conditions in New York, "Yom Kippur" is one of the most notable. It is the tale of a pious Jewish woman who joins her husband in America after he has been there several years. The details of the way in which she left the old country, how she had to pass herself off on the steamer as the wife of another man, her difficulties with the inspecting officers, etc., give the impression of a life strange to the Gentile world. On arriving in America, she finds her husband and his friends fallen away from the old faith. He had shaved off his beard, had grown to be slack about the *kosher* preparation of food and the observance of the religious holidays, he was no longer careful about the morning ablutions, worked on the Sabbath, and compelled her to take off the wig which every Orthodox Jewish woman must wear. She soon fell under the new influence and felt herself drifting generally into the ungodly ways of the New World. On the day of the great White Feast she found herself eating when she should have fasted. On Yom Kippur, the Day of Atonement, the sense of her sins overpowered her quite.

"Yom Kippur! Now the children of Israel are all massed together in every corner of the globe. They are congregated in synagogues and prayer houses, their eyes swollen with crying, their voices hoarse from wailing and supplicating, their broken hearts full of repentance. They all stand now in their funeral togas, like a throng of newly arisen dead."

She grows delirious and imagines that her father and mother come to her successively and reproach her for her degeneracy. In a series of frightful dreams, all bearing on her repentance, the atmosphere of the story is rendered so intense that her death, which follows, seems entirely natural.

The theme of one of Gorin's longer stories on Jewish-American life is of a young Jew who had married in the old country and had come to New York alone to make his fortune. If he had remained in Russia, he would have lived happily with his wife, but in America he acquired new ideas of life and new ideals of women and, therefore, felt alienated from her when she joined him in the New World. Many children came to them, his wages as a tailor diminished, and his wife grew constantly less congenial. He remained with her, however, from a sense of duty for eleven years, when, after insuring his life, he committed suicide.

## A SATIRIST OF TENEMENT SOCIETY

Leon Kobrin stands midway between Libin and Levin, on the one hand, and Gordin on the other. He carries his Russian traditions more intimately with him than do Libin and Levin, but more nearly approaches to a saturated exposition in fiction form of the life of Yiddish New York than does Gordin. Unlike the latter, he has the pretense rather than the reality of learning, and the reality rather than the pretense of realistic art. Yet he never quite attains to the untutored fidelity of Libin. Many of his sketches are satirical, some are rather burlesque descriptions of ghetto types, and some suggest the sad problem element which runs through Russian literature. He was born in Russia in 1872 of poor parents, Orthodox Jews, who sent him to the Hebrew school, of which the boy was never very fond—he preferred to read Russian at night surreptitiously. He found some good friends, who, as he put it, "helped me to the light through ghetto darkness." (Incidentally, it may be pointed out that the intellectual element of the Ghetto—the realists and socialists—think that progress is possible only in the line of Russian culture, and that to remain steadfast to Jewish traditions is to remain immersed in darkness.) So Kobrin struggled from a very early age to master the Russian language and even wrote sketches in that tongue. He, like Gordin, refers to the fact of his being a writer in Yiddish apologetically as something forced upon him by circumstances. Unlike Gorin, however, he believes in the literary capacity of the language, with which he was first impressed when he came to America in 1892 and found stories by Chekhov translated by Abraham Cahan and others into Yiddish and published in the *Arbeiterzeitung*. It was a long time, however, before Kobrin definitely identified himself with the literary calling. He first went through a course somewhat similar to that of the boy mathematician in the sketch by Libin, described above. He tried the sweatshop, but he was a bungler with the machines. Then he turned his hand with equal awkwardness to the occupation of making cigars, failed as distinctly as a baker and, finally, in 1894, was forced into literature and began writing for the *Arbeiterzeitung*.

One of Kobrin's sketches deals with a vulgar tailor of the East Side, who is painted in the ugliest of colors and is as disagreeable an individual as the hottest anti-Semite could imagine. The man, who is the boss of a sweatshop, meets the author in a suburban train, scrapes his acquaintance, fawns upon him, offers him a cigar, and tells about how well he is doing in New York. In Russia, where he had made clothes for rich people, no young girl would have spoken to him because of his low social position, but in the new country young women of good family abroad seek employment in his shop and are often dependent on him not only for a living but in more indescribable ways. Mr. Kobrin and his wife refer to this sketch as the "pig story."

A subtler tale is the picture of a domestic scene. Jake has returned from his work and sits reading a Yiddish newspaper. His wife, a passionate brunette, is working about the room, and every now and then glances at the apathetic Jake with a sigh. She remembers how it was a year ago, when Jake hung over her, devoted, attentive; now he goes out almost every evening to the "circle" and returns late. She tries to engage him in conversation, but he answers in monosyllables and finally says he is going out, whereupon she weeps and makes a scene. "He is not the same Jake," she cries bitterly. After some words intended to comfort her, but really rubbing in the wound, her husband goes to the "circle," and the wife burns the old love letters one by one; they are from another man, she feels, and are a torture to her now. As she burns the letters the tears fall and sizzle on the hot stove. It is a simple scene, but moving—what Mr. Kobrin calls "a small slice out of life."

An amusing couple of sketches, in which satire approaches burlesque, represent the infelicities of an old woman from Russia who had recently arrived in New York. One day, shocked at her children's neglect of a religious holiday and at their general unholiness, she goes to visit an old neighbor at whose house she is sure to have everything *kosher* and right. She has been accustomed to find the way to her friend by means of a wooden Indian, called by her a Turk, which stood before a tobacco shop. The Indian has been removed, however, and she consequently loses her way. Seeing a Jew with big whiskers who must, therefore, she thinks, be Orthodox, she asks him where the Turk is, and repeats the question in vain to many others, among them to a policeman, whom she addresses in Polish, for she thinks that all Gentiles speak that language, just as all Jews speak Yiddish. On another occasion the old lady goes to the theater, where her experiences are a Yiddish counterpart to those of Partridge at the play.

Some of the best sketches from life form portions of the plays which are produced at the Yiddish theaters on the Bowery. In the dramas of Gordin there are many scenes which far more faithfully than his newspaper sketches mirror the sordid life and unhappy problems of the poor Russian Jew in America, and the ability of the actors to enforce the theme and language by realistic dress, manner, and intonation makes these scenes frequently a genuine revelation to the Gentile of a new world of social conditions.

Kobrin and Libin, too, have written plays, very few and undramatic as compared with those of Gordin, but abounding in the sketch element, in scenes which give the setting and the milieu of a large and important section of humanity. The plays of Kobrin and Libin merely add more material to the same quality which runs through their newspaper sketches. Libin is the author of two plays, *The Belated Wedding* and *A Vain Sacrifice,* for which he was paid fifty dollars apiece. They are each a series of pictures from the miserable Jewish life in the New York ghetto. The latter play is the story of a girl who marries a man she hates in order to get money for her consumptive father. The theme of *The Belated Wedding* is too sordid to relate. Both plays are unrelieved gloom and lack any compensating dramatic quality. In Kobrin's plays—*The East Side Ghetto, East Broadway,* and *Broken Chains*—the problem element is more decided and the dramatic structure is more pronounced than in those of Libin. In *East Broadway* a young man and girl have been devoted to each other and to the cause of nihilism in Russia, but in New York the husband catches the spirit of the American businessman and demands from his father-in-law the money promised as a dot. The eloquence of the new point of view is opposed to that of the old in a manner not entirely undramatic.

The fact that there are a number of writers for the Yiddish newspapers of New York who are animated with a desire to give genuine glimpses of the real life of the people is particularly interesting, perhaps because of the light which it throws on the character of their Jewish readers and the breadth of culture which it implies. Certainly, there are many Russian Jews on the East Side who like to read anything which seems to them to be "natural," a word which is often on their lips. It would be misleading, however, to reach conclusions very optimistic in regard to the ghetto Jews as a whole, for the demand which makes these sketches possible is practically limited to the socialists, and grows less as that political and intellectual movement falls off, under American influences, in vitality. Today there are fewer good sketches published in the Yiddish newspapers than formerly, when the *Arbeiterzeitung* was a power for social and literary improvement. Quarrels among the socialists, resulting in many weakening splits, and the growth of a more constant commercial attitude on the part of the newspapers than formerly, are partly responsible for the change. The few men of talent who, under the stimulus of an editorial demand for sincere art, wrote in the early days with a full heart and entire conviction have now partly lost interest. Levin has given up writing altogether for the more remunerative work of a typesetter, Gorin has become largely a translator and literary hack on the regular newspaper staff, and Gordin and Kobrin have turned their attention to the writing of plays, for which there is a vital, if crude, demand. Libin alone, the most interesting and in a genuine way the most talented of them all, remains the poorest in worldly goods and the most devoted to his art.

# eight

# A NOVELIST

Although Abraham Cahan began his literary career as a Yiddish writer for the ghetto newspapers, his important work has been written and published in English. His work as a Yiddish writer was of an almost exclusively educational character. This at once establishes an important distinction between him and other Yiddish sketch writers. A still more vital distinction is that arising from the relative quality of his work, which, as opposed to that of the Yiddish writers, is more of the order of the story or of the novel than of the sketch. Cahan's work is more developed and more mature as art than that of the other men, who remain essentially sketch writers. Even in their longer stories what is good is the occasional flash of life, the occasional picture, and this does not imply characters and theme developed sufficiently to put them in the category of the novel. Rather than for the art they reveal, they are interesting for the sincere way in which they present a life intimately known. In fact the literary talent of the ghetto consists almost exclusively in the short sketch. To this general rule Abraham Cahan comes the nearest to forming an exception. Even in his work the sketch element predominates, but in one long story at least something more is successfully achieved. In his short stories there is often much circumstance and development, and he has now finished the first draft of a long novel. His stories have appeared from time to time in the leading English magazines, and there are two volumes with which the discriminating American and English public is familiar, *Yekl* and *The Imported Bridegroom and Other Stories*. As well as his work, Cahan's life too is of unusual interest. He had a picturesque career as a socialist and an editor in the ghetto.

Abraham Cahan was born in Vilnyus, the capital of Lithuania, Russia, in 1860. He went as a boy to the Jewish *chaider* but took an early and overpowering interest in the Russian language and ideas. He graduated from the teacher's institute at Vilnyus, and was appointed government teacher in the town of Velizh, Province of Vitebsk. Here he became interested, although not active, in the anarchistic doctrines which filled the intellectual atmosphere of the day, and, feeling that his liberty and activity were endangered by a longer sojourn in Russia, he came to America in 1882, when a time of severe poverty and struggle ensued.

From the first he, like most Russian Jews of intelligence, was identified with the socialist movement in the New York ghetto; he threw himself into it with extraordinary activity and soon became a leader in the quarter. He was an eloquent and impassioned speaker, went twice abroad as the American-Jewish delegate to socialist congresses, and was the most influential man connected with the weekly *Arbeiterzei-tung,* of which he became editor in 1893. This paper for several years carried on an aggressive warfare in the cause of labor and socialism, and attempted also to educate the people to an appreciation of the best realistic Russian writers, such as Tolstoy, Turgenev, and Chekhov. It was under Cahan's editorship of this weekly, and also of the monthly *Zukunft,* a journal of literature and social science, that some of the realistic sketch writers of the quarter discovered their talent, and for a time both literature and socialism were as vigorous as they were young in the colony.

Literature, however, was at that time to Cahan only the handmaiden of education. His career as an East Side writer was that primarily of the teacher. He wished not merely to educate the ignorant masses of the people in the doctrines of socialism, but to teach them the rudiments of science and literature. For that reason he wrote in Yiddish popularized science, wrote socialistic articles, and exhorted generally. Occasionally he published humorous sketches, intended, however, always to point a moral or convey some needed information. In literature, as such, he was not at that time interested as an author. It was only several years later, when he took up his English pen, that he attempted to put into practice the ideas about what constitutes the real literature to which he had been trying to educate the ghetto.

The fierce individualism which in spite of socialistic doctrine is a characteristic of the intellectual element in the ghetto soon brought about its weakening effects. The inevitable occurred. Quarrels grew among the socialists, the party was split, each faction organized a socialist newspaper, and the movement consequently lost in significance and general popularity. In 1896 Cahan resigned his editorship and retired, disgusted, from the work.

From that time on his interest in socialism waned, although he still ranges himself under that banner, and his other absorbing interest, realistic literature, grew apace, until it now absorbs everything else. As is the case with many imaginative and emotional men, he is predominantly of one intellectual passion. When he was an active socialist he wanted to be nothing else. He gave up his law studies and devoted himself to an unremunerative public work. When the fierce but small personal quarrels began which brought about the present confused condition of socialism in the ghetto, Cahan's always strong admiration for the Russian writers of genius and their literary school led him to experiment in the English language, which gave a field much larger than Yiddish. Always a reformer, always filled with some idea which he wished to propagate through the length and breadth of the land, Cahan took up the cause of realism in English fiction with the same passion and energy with which he had gone in for socialism. He became a partisan in literature just as he had been a partisan in active life. He admired among Americans W. D. Howells, who seemed to him to write in the proper spirit, but he felt that Americans as a class were hopelessly romantic, unreal, and undeveloped in their literary tastes and standards. He set himself to writing stories and books in English which should at least be genuine artistic transcripts from life, and he succeeded admirably in keeping out of his work any obvious doctrinaire element—which points to great artistic self-restraint when one considers how full of his doctrine the man is.

Love of truth, indeed, is the quality which seems to a stranger in the ghetto the great virtue of that section of the city. Truth, pleasant or unpleasant, is what the best of them desire. It is true that, in the reaction from the usual affable literature of the American book market, these realists rather prefer the unpleasant. That, however, is a sign of energy and youth. A vigorous youthful literature is always more apt to breathe the spirit of tragedy than a literature more mature and less fresh. And after all, the great passion of the intellectual quarter results in the consciously held and warmly felt principle that literature should be a transcript from life. Cahan represents this feeling in its purest aspect, and is therefore highly interesting not only as a man but as a type. This passion for truth is deeply infused into his literary work.

The aspects of the ghetto's life which would naturally hold the interest of the artistic observer are predominatingly its characteristic features—those qualities of character and conditions of social life which are different from the corresponding ones in the old country. Cahan came to America a mature man with the life of one community already a familiar thing to him. It was inevitable therefore that his literary work in New York should have consisted largely in fiction emphasizing the changed character and habits of the

Russian Jew in New York, describing the conditions of immigration, and depicting the clash between the old and the new ghetto and the way the former insensibly changes into the latter. In this respect Cahan presents a great contrast to the simple Libin, who merely tells in a heartfelt passionate way the life of the poor sweatshop Jew in the city, without consciously taking into account the relative nature of the phenomena. Libin's work is absolute work as far as it goes, as straight and true as an arrow, and implies no knowledge of other conditions. Cahan presents an equally striking contrast to the work of men like Gordin and Gorin, the best part of which deals with Russian rather than New York life.

If Cahan's work were merely the transcribing in fiction form of a great number of suggestive and curious points about the life of the poor Russian Jew in New York, it would not of course have any great interest to even the cultivated Anglo-Saxon reader, who, though he might find the stories curious and amusing for a time, would recognize nothing in them sufficiently familiar to be of deep importance to him. If, in other words, the stories had lacked the universal element always present in true literature, they would have been of very little value to anyone except the student of queer corners. When however the universal element of art is present, when the special conditions are rendered sympathetic by the touch of common human nature, the result is pleasing in spite of the foreign element; it is even pleasing because of that element, for then the pleasure of easily understanding what is unfamiliar is added to the charm of recognizing the old objects of the heart and the imagination.

Cahan's stories may be divided into two general classes: those presenting primarily the special conditions of the ghetto to which the story and characters are subordinate, and those in which the special conditions and the story fuse together and mutually help and explain one another. These two—the information element and the human nature element—struggle for the mastery throughout his work. In the most successful part of the stories, the human nature element masters, without suppressing, that of special information.

The substance of Cahan's stories, what they have deliberately to tell us about the New York ghetto, is, considering the limited volume of his work, rich and varied. It includes the description of much that is common to the Jews of Russia and the Jews of New York—the picture of the Orthodox Jew, the pious rabbi, the marriage customs, the religious holidays, etc. But the Orthodox foreign element is treated more as a background on which are painted in contrasting lights the moral and physical forms resulting from the particular colonial conditions. The falling away of the children in filial respect and in religious faith; the consequent despair of the parents who are influenced only in superficial ways by their new environment, the alienation of progressive husbands from old-fashioned wives, the institution of the boarder (a source of frequent domestic trouble); the tendency of the new daughters of Israel to select husbands for themselves in spite of ancient authority and the *ver-*

*mittler* and their ambition to marry doctors and lawyers instead of Talmudical scholars; the professional
letter writers through whom ignorant people in the
old country and their ignorant relatives here corre-
spond; the falling-off in respect for the Hebrew
scholar and the rabbi; the tendency to read in the Astor Library and do other dreadful things implying interest in American life, to eat *treife* food, talk American slang, and hate being called a greenhorn (*i.e.,* an
old-fashioned Jew); how a *mister* in Russia becomes
a *shister* (shoemaker) in New York, and a *shister* in
Russia becomes a *mister* in New York; how women
lay aside their wigs and men shave their beards and
ride in horsecars on Saturday. All these things and
more are told in more or less detail in Cahan's English stories. Anyone who followed the long series of
barge-office sketches, which during the last few years
Cahan has published anonymously in the *Commercial Advertiser,* would be familiar in a general way
with the different types of Jews who come to this
country, with the reasons for their immigration and
the conditions which confront them when they arrive. Many of these hastily conceived and written
newspaper reports—they have plenty of life and
flashes of humor and pathos—are quick, rather
formless and contain a great deal of implicit literature. But the salient quality of this division of Cahan's work is the amount of strange and picturesque
information which it conveys.

Many of his more carefully executed stories, which
have appeared from time to time in the magazines,
are loaded down with a like quantity of information,

and while all of them have marked vitality, many are less intrinsically interesting, from the point of view of human nature, than even the barge-office sketches.

A marked instance of a story in which the information element overpoweringly predominates is "The Daughter of Reb Avrom Leib," published in the *Cosmopolitan Magazine* for May, 1900. The tale opens with a picture of Aaron Zalkin, who is lonely. It is Friday evening, and for the first time since he left his native town he enters a synagogue. Then we have a succession of minutely described customs and objects which are interesting in themselves and convey no end of local color. We learn that orthodox Jewish women have wigs, we read of the holy ark, the golden shield of David, the illuminated *omud*, the reading platform in the center, the faces of the worshipers as they hum the Song of Songs, and then the cantor and the cantor's daughter. We follow the cantor in his ceremonies and prayers. Zalkin is thrilled by the ceremony and thrilled by the girl. But only a word is given to him before the story goes back to picturing the scene, Reb Avrom Leib's song, and the actions of the congregation. In the second division of the story Zalkin goes again the next Friday night to the synagogue, and the result is that he wants to marry the girl. So he sends a marriage agent to the cantor, the girl's father. Then he goes to view the bride, and incidentally we learn that the cantor has two sons who are "American boys" and "will not turn their tongues to a Hebrew word." When the old man finds that Zalkin is a Talmudic scholar, he is startled and delighted and wants him for a son-in-law. They try to outquote one another, shouting and gesticulating "in true Talmudic fashion." There is a short scene between the two young people, the wedding day is deferred till the Nine Days are over, for "who would marry while one was mourning the Fall of the Temple?" And it is suggested that Sophie is not quite content. Then there is a scene where Zalkin chants the Prophets, where the betrothal articles ("a mixture of Chaldaic and Hebrew") are read, and a plate is thrown on the floor to make a severance of the ceremony "as unlikely as would be the reunion of the broken plate." Then there are more quotations from the cantor, a detailed picture of the services of the Day of Atonement, of the Rejoicing of the Law, of the blessing of the Dedication Lights, of the Days of Awe, and of the Rejoicing of the Law again. The old man's character is made very vivid, and the dramatic situation—that of a Jewish girl who, after the death of her father, marries in compliance with his desire—is picturesquely handled. But the theme is very slight. Most of the detail is devoted to making a picture, not of the changing emotions in the characters and the development of the human story, but of the religious customs of the Jews. The emphasis is put on information rather than on the theme, and consequently the story does not hold the interest strongly.

Many of Cahan's other short stories suffer because of the learned intention of the author. We derive a great deal of information and we generally get the picture, but it often requires an effort to keep the attention fixed on what is unfamiliar and at the same time so apart from the substance of the story that it is merely subordinate detail.

In these very stories, however, there is much that is vigorous and fresh in the treatment and characterization, and a vein of lyric poetry is frequent, as in the delightful *Ghetto Wedding*, the story of how a poor young Jewish couple spend their last cent on an elaborate wedding feast, expecting to be repaid by the presents, and thus enabled to furnish their apartment. The gifts don't turn up, only a few guests are present, and the young people, after the ceremony, go home with nothing but their enthusiastic love. The naïveté and simplicity of the lovers, the implicit sympathy with them, and a kind of gentle satire, make this little story a gem for the poet.

*The Imported Bridegroom* is a remarkable character sketch and contains several very strong and interesting descriptions. Asriel Stroon is the central figure and lives before the mind of the reader. He is an old Jew who has made a business success in New York and retired, when he has a religious awakening and at the same time a great longing for his old Russian home, Pravly. He goes back to Pravly on a visit, and the description of his sensations the day he returns to his home is one of the best examples of the essential vitality of Cahan's work. This long story contains also a most amusing scene where Asriel outbids a famous rich man of the town for a section in the synagogue and triumphs over him, too, in the question of a son-in-law. There is in Pravly a prodigy of holiness and Talmudic learning, Shaya, whom Reb Lippe wants for his daughter, but Asriel wants him too and, being enormously rich, carries him off in triumph to his daughter in America. But Flora at first spurns him. He is a "greenhorn," a scholar, not a smart American doctor such as she has dreamed of. Soon, however, Shaya, who is a great student, learns English and mathematics, and promises Flora to become a doctor. The first thing he knows he is a freethinker and an American, and Flora now loves him. They keep the terrible secret from the old man, but he ultimately sees Shaya going into the Astor Library and eating food in a *treife* restaurant. His resentment is pathetic and intense but the children marry, and the old man goes to Jerusalem with his faithful servant.

The book, however, in which there is a perfect adaptation of atmosphere and information to the dramatic story, is *Yekl*. In this strong, fresh work, full of buoyant life, the ghetto characters and environment form an integral part.

*Yekl* indeed ought to be well-known to the English reading public. It is a book written and conceived in the English language, is essentially idiomatic and consequently presents no linguistic difficulties. It gives a great deal of information about what seems to me by far the most interesting section of foreign New York. But what ought to count more than anything else is that it is a genuine piece of literature, picturing characters that live in art, in an environment that is made real, by means of a story that is vital and significant and that never flags in interest. In its quality of freshness and buoyancy it recalls the work of Turgenev. None of Cahan's later work, though most of it has vital elements, stands in the same class with this fundamentally sweet piece of literature. It takes a worthy place with the best Russian fiction, with that school of writers who make life actual by the sincere handling of detail in which the simple everyday emotions of unspoiled human nature are portrayed. The English classic novel, greatly superior in the rounded and contemplative view of life, has yet nothing since Fielding comparable to Russian fiction in vivid presentation of the details of life. This whole school of literature can, I believe, be compared in quality more fittingly with Elizabethan drama than with anything which has intervened in English literature, not of course with those maturer dramas in which there is a great philosophical treatment of human life, but in the lyric freshness and imaginative vitality which were common to the whole lot of Elizabethan writers.

*Yekl* is alive from beginning to end. The virtuosity in description, which in Cahan's work sometimes takes the place of literature, is here quite subordinate. Yekl is a sweatshop Jew in New York who has left a wife and child in Russia in order to make a little home for them and himself in the New World. In the early part of the book he is becoming an "American" Jew, making a little money and taking a great fancy to the smart Jewish girl who wears a rakish hat and no wig, talks "United States," and has a profound contempt for the benighted pious greenhorns who have just arrived. A sweatshop girl named Mamie moves his fancy deeply, so that when the faithful wife Gitl and the little boy Yossele arrive at the barge office

*"Yekl"*

there is evidently trouble at hand. At that place Yekl
meets them in a vividly told scene—ill-concealed dis-
quiet on his part and naive alarm at the situation on
hers. Gitl's wig and her subdued, old-fashioned demeanor tell terribly on Yekl's nerves, and she is
shocked by everything that happens to her in America. Their domestic unhappiness develops through a
number of characteristic and simple incidents until

it results in a divorce. But by that time Gitl is becoming "American" and it is obvious that she is to be taken care of by a young man in the quarter more appreciative than Yekl. The latter finds himself bound to Mamie, the pert "American" girl, and as the book closes is in a fair way to regret the necessity of giving up his newly acquired freedom. This simple,

"Yekl"

strong theme is treated consistently in a vital presentative way. The idea is developed by natural and constant incident, psychological or physical, rather than by talk. Every detail of the book grows naturally out of the situation.

"Unpleasant" is a word which many an American would give to *Yekl* on account of its subject. Strong compensating qualities are necessary to induce a publisher or editor to print anything which they think is in subject disagreeable to the big body of American readers, most of whom are women. Without attempting to criticize the voice of the people, it may be pointed out that there are at least two ways in which a book may be "unpleasant." It may be so in the formal theme, the characters, the result—things may come out unhappily, vice triumphant, and the section of life portrayed may be a sordid one. This is the kind of unpleasantness which publishers particularly object to; and in this sense *Yekl* may fairly be called "unpleasant." Turgenev's *Torrents of Spring* is also in this sense "unpleasant," for it tells how a young man's sincere and poetic first love is turned to failure and misery by the illegitimate temporary attraction of a fascinating woman of the world. But Turgenev's novel is nevertheless full of buoyant vitality, full of freshness and charm, of youth and grace, full of life-giving qualities—because of it we all may live more abundantly. The same may be said of many another book. When there is sweetness, strength, and early vigor in a book, the reader is refreshed, notwithstanding the theme. And it is noticeable that youth is not afraid of subjects.

Another way in which a book may be "unpleasant" is in the quality of deadness. Many books with pleasant and moral themes and endings are unpoetic and unpleasantly mature. Even a book great in subject, with much philosophy in it, may show a lack of sensitiveness to the vital qualities, to the effects of spring, to the joy in mere physical life, which are so marked and so genuinely invigorating in the best Russian fiction. The extreme of this kind of unpleasantness is shown in the case of some modern Frenchmen and Italians, not primarily in the theme, but in the lack of poetry and vigor, of hope, in a sodden maturity, often indeed combined with great qualities of intellect and workmanship, but dead to the little things of life, dead to the feeling of spring in the blood, to naive readiness for experience. An American who is the antithesis of this kind of thing is Walt Whitman. His quality put into prose is what we have in the best Russian novels. In the latter acceptation of the word "unpleasant," too, it cannot be applied to *Yekl*, for *Yekl* is youthful and vital. There is buoyant spring in the lines and robust joy in truth whatever it may be.

Apropos of Cahan's love of truth, and the word "unpleasant," a discussion which took place a few years ago on the appearance of Zangwill's play, *The Children of the Ghetto,* is illuminative. That poetic drama represented the life of the poor ghetto Jew with sympathy and truth, but for that very reason it was severely criticized by some uptown Israelites. Many of these, no doubt, had religious objections to a display on the stage of those customs and observances of their race which touched upon the "holy Law." But some of the rich German Jews, practically identified with American life and desiring for practical and social purposes to make little of their racial distinction, deprecated literature which portrayed the life of those Jews who still have distinctively national traits and customs. Then, too, there is a tendency among the well-to-do American Jews to look down upon their ghetto brethren, to regard the old customs as benighted, and to treat them with a certain contempt—although they spend a great deal of charitable money in the quarter. Feeling a little ashamed of the poor Russian East Side Jew, they object to a serious literary portrayal of him. They want no attention called to what they deem the less attractive aspects of their race. An uptown Jewish lady, on the appearance in a newspaper of a story about East Side Jewish life, wrote a protesting letter to the editor. She told the writer of the sketch, when he was sent to see her, that she could not see why he didn't write about uptown Jews instead of sordid East Side Jews. The scribe replied that he wrote of the ghetto Jew because he found him interesting, while he couldn't see anything attractive or picturesque about the comfortable Israelite uptown.

Abraham Cahan's stories have been subjected to criticism inspired by the same spirit. Feeling the charm of his people he has attempted to picture them as they are, in shadow and light, and has consequently been accused of betraying his race to the Gentiles.

The attitude of the East Side Jews toward writers

like Zangwill and Cahan is in refreshing contrast. The Yiddish newspapers were enthusiastic about *The Children of the Ghetto*, in which they felt the Jews were truthfully and therefore sympathetically portrayed. In the literary sketches and plays now produced in considerable numbers in Yiddish, a great pride of race is manifest. The writers have not lost their self-respect, still abound in their own sense, and are consequently vitally interesting. They are full of ideals and enthusiasm and do not object to what is "unpleasant" so strenuously as do their uptown brethren.

---

The first to occupy the Lower East Side were the Yankees. The Yankees named all the streets—Eldridge, Delancey, Orchard, Forsythe, Houston, Allen. After the Yankees, the Germans came and then the Irish, followed by the Bohemians, the Jews, the Russians, the Greeks, the Italians, the Poles, with a smattering of other races. Each left behind a reminder of its presence. The colonial Yankees left their cemetery, which was in the heart of the ghetto I knew as a boy. This was the old Marble Cemetery on Second Street and Second Avenue that fascinated all the young Jewish boys. Here rested the bodies of old New Yorkers—John Ericsson, who built the *Monitor* in the Civil War (I think his body was later moved to his native country). Here was the grave of President James Monroe with the marker indicating that the body had been removed to his native Virginia. This was all a Protestant stronghold once, then Roman Catholic, then Jewish, and now the Negroes make it Protestant again.

In 1908 the illuminated cross on the steeple of St. Augustine's Chapel on Houston Street dominated the ghetto. It could be seen for blocks against the deep night sky, forever a fixture in our minds.

A half-mile up Second Avenue was St. Mark's Lutheran Church. Everybody on the East Side knew the story that the body of A. T. Stewart, founder of Wanamaker's Department Store, had been stolen from its resting place in the church's graveyard.

Later the entire East Side went into mourning because of the great tragedy that afflicted St. Mark's Lutheran Church. The parish lost most of its children in a terrible disaster when the *Slocum,* a holiday ship, caught fire. Many of the children who jumped overboard were caught by the big knife-like paddles of the excursion boat. The Jewish organizations marched in the St. Mark's funeral procession.

Second Avenue was the Great White Way of the Lower East Side, a promenade for the young people. On Sunday afernoons it was a gay sight. Up this street we sold our newspapers as newsboys among the thousands of factory workers who poured out of the tenements in the morning, all moving toward the clothing factories and department stores beyond Union Square.

On the corner of Second Avenue and Fourteenth Street was the Labor Temple. I remember the signs LECTURE TONIGHT that daily announced the evening's activities. I heard Margaret Sanger there, Will Durant, and Clarence Darrow. The Labor Temple was founded by Charles Stelze, a Presbyterian clergyman, one of the many Christians who worked among Jewish immigrants to help them into the open society of America. Frances Perkins came to the East Side early, as did Eleanor Roosevelt and Mrs. O. H. P. Belmont, and I remember volunteer social workers from the fashionable St. Thomas's Episcopal Church on Fifth Avenue.

# nine

# THE YOUNG ART
# AND ITS EXPONENTS

On Hester Street, east of the Bowery, the poor Jew is
revealed in many a characteristic way. It is the home
of the sweatshop, of the crowded tenement house.
Old peddlers, as ragged as the poorest beggars, stand
on street corners. In long uninterrupted lines are the
carts containing fruit, cake, dry goods, fish—everything that the proletarian Jew requires. Behind these
tower the crowded tenement houses, with fire escapes
for balconies. Through the middle of the street constantly moves a mass of people. No vehicle can go
rapidly there, for the thoroughfare is literally alive.
In the least crowded part of the day, however, tattered little girls may sometimes be seen dancing with
natural grace to the music of a hand organ, the Italian owner of which for some strange reason, has em-
bedded himself in the very heart of poverty. Between
the lumbering wagons which infest the street at the
less busy part of the day these little children wonder-
fully sway and glide and constitute the only gladsome
feature of the scene. Just as Canal Street, with its
cafés where the poets, socialists, scholars, and jour-

nalists meet, is the mind of the ghetto, so Hester Street represents its heart. This picturesque street has recently become the study of several young Jewish artists.

---

Because tenements were crowded and dirty and dark the real life of the ghetto was in the street. When we got up in the morning we went out—to work, to the factories, to the trucks, to the school. In the summertime we simply went out on the streets. Everybody was in the street. The old folks sat on the stoop of the tenement building and the boys and girls played on the street. The one salient impression I retain about the Lower East Side of New York is children, vast numbers of children, or, as the elderly Jews said, children underfoot. The Jews were fruitful and multiplied. They were spiting Pharaoh. The idea of spiting Pharaoh was no more remote from our minds than the idea that George Washington was the father of our country. The whole thing was like yesterday. I have always been thrilled by the idea that the Jews have been contemporaneous with all recorded history.

It has been forty-seven years that I've been out of there, but I doubt seriously whether a single month has passed without my thinking of the children, the little Italian girls dancing the tarantella to the music of the organ grinder, the little Jewish girls playing potsy on the street while they kept an eye on infant brothers. I have memories of the early morning on the East Side during the summertime when I went to pick up the early edition of the *Jewish Morning Journal* at six in the morning at the moment the boys coming out of the tenements were on their way to the synagogue to say their early-morning *Kaddish* for a departed parent.

The street meant a good deal to us. Each summer we had a contest growing grass between the cracks in the sidewalk. We counted the blades of grass, and the one

*A little girl of Hester Street*

who had more blades in the crack on the sidewalk won. I don't think there was a prize.

I do not want to give the impression that we were all "good" boys. We had bad ones. We had boys who wound up in Sing Sing, some made it all the way to the death house. Tourists rode through the area on what we called "rubberneck" wagons and buses. The guides promised to show them the "dens" of East Side gunmen and white slavers. The gullible tourists gripped their seats in ecstasy as the megaphone fellow pointed out these infamous and notorious places. The East Side contributed its share of criminals, prostitutes, procurers, and pickpockets—but no more than its share. The worst part of New York in those days was the middle of the city—the Tenderloin on the West Side, where they needed seven policemen for every one they needed in the ghetto (according to New York police department records, 1906-07).

The East Side's chief crime was poverty. Its chief virtue was the drive to make good.

The last few years have brought the earliest indications of what may develop into a characteristic ghetto art. In the course of their long civilization the Jews have never developed a national plastic art. Devoted to the things of the spirit, in an important period of their history in conflict with the sensuous art of the Greeks, they have never put into external forms the heart of their life. There have been occasional painters and sculptors among them, but these have worked in line with the Gentiles, and have in no way contributed to a typical or national art. With the slackening of the Hebraic religion, however, which

*Hester Street pushcarts at night*

prohibits images in the temple—that fertile source of inspiration in Christian art—the conditions have been more favorable, and the beginning of a distinctive ghetto art has already made its appearance in New York.

On the corner of Hester and Forsyth streets is a tumble-down rickety building. The stairs that ascend to the garret are pestiferous and dingy. In what is more like a shed than a room, with the wooden ribs of the slanting roof curtailing the space, is the studio of an East Side artist. A miserable iron bedstead occupies the narrow strip of floor beneath the descending ceiling. There is one window, which commands a good view of the pushcart market in Hester Street. Near the window is a diminutive oil stove, on which the artist prepares his tea and eggs. On a peg on the door hang an old mackintosh and an extra coat—his only additional wardrobe. About the narrow walls on the three available sides are easels, and sketches and paintings of ghetto types.

Jacob Epstein, the artist, has a melancholy, wistful face. He was born in the ghetto twenty years ago of poor Jews, who were at first tailors and afterward small trades-people, and who had emigrated from Poland. He went to the public schools until he was thirteen years old. Since then he has worked at various jobs. Until recently he was an instructor in the boys' outdoor gymnasium near the corner of Hester and Essex. For one summer, in order to get a vacation, he became a farm laborer. His art education, as well as his education in general, is slight, consisting of two terms at the Art Students' League. But for so young a man his intellectual, as well as his artistic activity, has been considerable. He belongs to a number of debating societies, and is now hesitating in his mind whether to become a socialist or an anarchist, although he is tending toward a humane socialism.

Two things, however, he seems definitely to have settled—that he will devote himself to his art, and that that art shall be the plastic picturing of the life of his people in the ghetto. He seems to rejoice at having lost his various potboiling positions.

"I was not a gymnast," he said cheerfully, explaining why he left the last one, "and now they have a gymnast."

Now he lives alone on his beloved Hester Street in the studio, where he sleeps and eats. For that modest room he pays four dollars a month, and, as he cooks his own meals, twelve dollars a month is quite sufficient to satisfy all his needs. This amount he can usually manage to make through the sale of his sketches; but when he does not he "goes to bed," as he puts it, and lies low until one of his various little art enterprises brings him in a small check. Withal, he is very happy, although serious, like his race in general, and full of idealism and ambition. On one occasion the idea occured to him and to his friend, Bernard Gussow, that men ought to live closer to nature than they can in the ghetto. It was in the wintertime that they were filled with this conviction, but they nevertheless packed off and hired a farmhouse at Greenwood Lake and stayed there the whole winter. When their money gave out, they cut ice in the river to pay the rent.

"We enjoyed it very much," said Epstein, "but there were no artistic results. The country, much as I love it, is not stimulating. Clouds and trees are not satisfying. It is only in the ghetto, where there is human nature, that I have ideas for sketches."

With a kind of regret the artist spoke of the beauty of Winslow Homer's landscape. He called it "epic," and was filled with sorrow that such an art could not be in the ghetto.

"There is no nature in the sweatshop," he said, "and yet it is there and in the crowded street that my love and my imagination call me. It is only the minds and souls of my people that fill me with a desire to work."

It is this ambition which makes Jacob Epstein and the other young artists to be mentioned of uncommon representative interest. Epstein is filled with a melancholy love of his race, and his constant desire is to paint his people just as they are—to show them in their suffering picturesqueness. So he goes into the sweatshop and sketches, induces the old peddlers of Hester Street to pose in his studio, and draws from his window the pushcarts and the old women in the street. It is thus a characteristic ghetto art, an art dealing with the peculiar types of that Jewish community, that Epstein's interest leads to—a national plastic art, as it were, on a small scale.

In the studio and at an exhibition at the Hebrew Institute, Epstein had two years ago a number of sketches and a few paintings—the latter very crude as far as the technique of color is concerned, and the sketches in charcoal rough and showing compara-

Jacob Epstein's "A Type of Laboring Man" is a fellow I saw many times. I recognized his face. I sold newspapers on certain days on East Broadway, a distance of two city blocks from the chazar (pig) market, where the working men stood around with symbols of their trade.

Jacob Epstein's fellow was holding a saw in his hand and carrying the tools of the carpenter in a bag over his shoulder. I remember him well. There were other fellows with panes of glass under their arms to show that they were glaziers, and here and there a man held up a hammer or a piece of lead pipe. Folks came to the chazar market and picked out the mechanic they needed. They made their deal right there.

In recent years I've seen the same "market" in the South —Negroes standing around, usually near the railroad station. Most of the Negroes are unskilled, however, and do not carry tools of a trade. They are laborers and janitors for odd jobs. The folks come in their automobiles and take them away. They, too, make their deal on the spot as did the folks in the ghetto chazar market on the edge of Seward Park, where I heard Charles Evans Hughes deliver a campaign speech in his contest with President Wilson in 1916.

tively slight mastery of the craft. But, particularly in the sketches, there is character in every one, and at once a sympathetic and a realistic imagination. He tells the truth about the ghetto as he sees it, but into the dark reality of the external life he puts frequently a melancholy beauty of spirit. Portraits of old peddlers, roughly successful as ghetto types, whom in order to retain as models the artist was frequently forced to sing a song, for the peddlers have a Jewish horror of the image, and it is difficult to get them to pose: one of them with an irregular, blunted nose and eyes sad and plaintive, but very gentle; an old Jew in the synagogue praying "Holy, Holy"; many sweatshop scenes, gaunt figures half-dressed, with enormously long arms and bony figures; mothers working in the shops with babies in their arms; one woman, tired, watching for a moment her lean husband working the machine (that machine of which Morris Rosenfeld sings so powerfully in "The Sweat Shop"); a woman with her head leaning heavily on her hands; Hester Street market scenes, with dreary tenement houses—a kind of prison wall—as background; one peddler with a sensitive face—a man the artist had to catch at odd times, surreptitiously, for, religious to an extreme, the old fellow would hastily trundle off whenever he saw Epstein.

A characteristic of this young artist's work is the seriousness with which he tries to get the type as it is, the manifest love involved in the way it takes his imagination. With his whole soul he hates caricature of his race. Most of the magazine illustrations of ghetto characters he finds distorted and untrue, many of them, however, done with a finish of technique that he envies. A big and ugly nose is not Epstein's idea of what constitutes a downtown Jew. The Jew, to him, is recognized rather by the peculiar melancholy of the eyes. In the nose he sees nothing particularly typical of the race. It is a forcible illustration of how, while really remaining faithful to the external type, his love for the race leads him to emphasize the spiritual and humane expressiveness of the faces about him, and so paves the way to an art imaginative as well as typical, not lacking even in a certain ideal beauty.

Bernard Gussow, Epstein's friend and fellow worker in the attempt to found a distinctive ghetto art, is in a still earlier stage of development. His essays in the plastic reproduction of Hester Street types are not yet as humanly interesting as those of the younger man, who, however, has been working longer and more assiduously. It is only for the past year or two that Gussow has definitely espoused this cause.

Unlike Epstein, he was not born in New York. The town of Slutzk, in the government of Ulinsk, Russia, is his birthplace, where he stayed until he was eleven years old. His father is a teacher of Hebrew, and young Gussow consequently received a much better education than Epstein, and also became much more familiar with the religious life of the Orthodox Jews. For that reason Epstein urges his friend to take the New York Orthodox synagogue and the domestic life of the religious Jew as his distinctive field in the great work in hand. For this, too, Gussow hopes, but in the present condition of his technique he limits himself to Hester Street scenes.

In New York, Gussow continued to build up an education uncommonly good in the ghetto. He went through high school, entered the city college, which he left for art school, and spent one season at the Art Students' League and two at the Academy of Design. He has for many years given lessons in English, to which occupation he, unlike his more emotional friend, prudently holds on. But Gussow, also, is deeply if not emotionally interested in the life of the ghetto, and in a broader if less intense form than is Epstein. With the contemporary Yiddish literature and journalism of New York he is well acquainted. His mind is more conservative and judicial than that of Epstein, but his sketches lack, at present at least, the touch of strong sympathy and imagination which is marked in the art of the younger man.

Gussow lives with his father's family, where he keeps his sketches. But to work, he goes to a room on the corner of Hester and Essex streets occupied by a poor Jewish family. Here the artist sits by the window and watches the poor and picturesque scenes in the big pushcart market directly beneath him. The subjects of his sketches are roughly the same as those of Epstein, although he draws rather more from the street and Epstein from the sweatshop. Groups standing about the pushcarts, examining goods and bargaining; an old woman with a cheese in her hand and an enormous nose (which Epstein reproachfully calls a caricature); several sketches representing men or women holding eggs to the sun, as a test preliminary to buying; carpenters waiting on the corner near the market for a job; an old Jew critically examining apples; a roughly indicated, rather attractive Jewish girl; a woman standing by a pushcart counting her money; a confused Hester Street crowd, walled in by the lofty tenement houses; a wall painter with an interesting face, who peddles horse radish when not occupied with painting; a peddler out of work, just from the hospital, his beard straggling in again, with the characteristic sad eyes of his race—this rather small list comprises the greater part of Gussow's work, and most of it is of a distinctly sketchy nature.

"You see," said Epstein sympathetically, "Bernard has until recently been working for the tenement house committee, and has only just got away from his job." Both of these young men seem to think it a piece of good luck when they are discharged by their employers.

These artists both recognize that the distinctive ghetto art is in its earliest stage; and that whatever has yet been done in that direction is technically very imperfect. But they call attention even to the crayon art stores of the ghetto as crudely pointing in the right direction. In those chromos, which contain absolutely no artistic quality, is represented, nevertheless, the religious and domestic life of the Jews and their physical types. And whatever art there is at present is supported by the popularity with the people of this crayon work. On the basis of that, the artist proper may work out the type into more truly interpretative forms.

For this young art, the object of which is to give a realistic picture of the life of the ghetto, it is easy to conceive an unduly sentimental interest. It is not unnatural in this time of great attention to East Side charitable work to give greater value than it deserves to an art which represents the sordidness and the pathos of that part of the city. Against this attitude, which they also call sentimental, Epstein and Gussow earnestly protest, and maintain that unless the ghetto art becomes some day technically excellent it will have no legitimate value. They want it judged on the same basis that any other art is judged, and they are filled with the faith, or at least the enthusiastic Epstein is, that the time will come when the artists of the ghetto will paint typical Jewish life, and paint it technically well.

It is true, of course, that the ultimate value of this little art movement in the ghetto will depend upon how well the attempt to paint the life is eventually carried out. But, nevertheless, even if nothing comes of it, it is important as suggesting an interesting departure from what is the prevailing limitation of American art. In Epstein's work something of the typical life of a community is expressed. Of what American painter from among the Gentiles can this be said? Where is the typical, the nationally characteristic, in our art? Our best painters experiment with all kinds of subjects. They put talent, sometimes genius, into their work, but at the basis of it there is no simple presentation of well-recognized and deeply felt national or even sectional life— merely essays in art, of more or less skill, showing no warm interest in any one kind of life.

There are many other artists, besides these two, in the ghetto, some of whom also occasionally paint a distinctive ghetto type. But for the most part trained as they have been in the uptown art schools, they experiment with all sorts of subjects in the approved American style. They paint girls in white and girls in blue, etc. (as Epstein expressed it scornfully) and put no general ghetto quality into their work. They do not seem deeply interested in anything except painting. Many of them are technically better educated than Epstein and Gussow, though it is probably safe to say that no one of them has the sympathetic imagination of Epstein. It is to this eclectic, experimental tendency of the artists in the ghetto in general that Epstein and Gussow present a contrast—in their love of their people and their desire to paint them as they are.

A typical representative of this less centered art is Samuel Kalisch, twenty-six years old, who came to this country from Austria twelve years ago. Older than the two young enthusiasts, Kalisch has had more experience and has developed a more efficient technique. He works in oils to a greater extent than the others and has a number of comparatively finished pictures; but his studio resembles that of any rather undistinguished uptown artist in point of diversity of subject and artistic impulse. There is an Oriental scene of conventional character; a portrait of himself taken from the mirror; a number of examples of still life apples and flowers, a cute scene of children playing on the beach; a landscape, etc. Of distinctive ghetto things, there are two old men, one just from the synagogue, with pensive eyes, a long beard and a derby hat, the other, ninety-four years old, sits in the synagogue, with a long white beard, a black cap on his head, a cane in one hand, and the Talmud in the other. These two portraits show considerable technical skill, but are faithful rather than interpretative, and indicate that the artist's sympathy is not absorbed in the life of the ghetto. They are merely subjects, like any other, which might come to his hand.

Now in full sympathy with what may be called the movement is Nathaniel Loewenberg, a little, black-haired, sad-eyed, sensitive, and appealing Russian Jew of twenty-one years of age. It is only recently however, that he has turned from landscape to city types, of which he has a few sketches, very incomplete with one exception, that also unfinished but unusually promising. It is in oil and represents a Jewish fish peddler of attractive countenance and shabby clothes trying to sell a fine fish to three ghetto women, these latter cleverly distinguished—one who will probably buy, another who apparently would like to if she could reduce the price, and the third indifferent.

Loewenberg was born in Moscow, of parents who were then and are now in business. He is enthusiastic at present over two things—Russian literature and the life of the Jews. On his table are two books—

one a history of the Hebrews, the other Tolstoy's *Awakening* in Russian. His newest interest is the ghetto, "for," he said, "the ghetto is full of character. There the people's life is more exposed than anywhere else, and the artist can easily penetrate into it."

The type Loewenberg hopes to delineate is of different character from that of Hester Street, where Gussow and Epstein work. His field is mainly at the corner of Rivington and Attorney streets, where the Jews are Hungarians and Poles and have a distinctive type. That is the location of another pushcart market, and although the human types are different from those of Hester Street, the peddling occupations are identical. Loewenberg's fancy runs largely to the young Jewish girl of this quarter, and she is represented in several half-done sketches.

The New York ghetto is constantly changing. It shifts from one part of town to another, and the time is not so very far distant when it will cease to exist altogether. The sweatshop will happily disappear with advancing civilization in New York. The tenement houses will change in character, the Jewish children will learn English and partly forget their language and customs. In spite of the fact that the Jews have been at all times and in all countries tenacious of their domestic peculiarities and their religion, the special character of the ghetto will pass away in favorably conditioned America. The picturesqueness it now possesses will disappear. Perhaps, by that time, however, an art will have been developed which will preserve for future generations the character of the present life, which may thus have historical value and artistic beauty in addition. Epstein and Gussow, devoted to this result as they are, are yet quite eager to see present conditions pass away. To them the art they have selected seems of trifling importance in comparison with a general improvement of the people they seem genuinely to love. They would be glad to have the present picturesqueness of the ghetto give place to conditions more analogous to those of happier sections of New York.

But in the meantime these few young artists, two or three particularly interested in ghetto types, five or six others, perhaps more who occasionally contribute a sketch of the ghetto, are in a fair way to get together a considerable body of pictures which shall have the distinction of portraying the Jewish community of the East Side with fair adequacy. Certainly the interest of that Hester Street life, and of the tenement houses that line it, is deep enough to inspire some serious man of plastic genius. And then it is not improbable that some great somber pictures will be painted. The conditions for such a significant art are ripe, and it may find its master in one or another of the young men who are passionately "doing" Hester Street.

---

It is interesting that Jacob Epstein, steeped in Orthodoxy which abhors the graven image, should become the great sculptor of the century.

The drawings he made for this book were his first published work. Raised on the Lower East Side, Epstein was fascinated by its swarming life. When his family moved out, he kept a room on Hester Street from which he might continue to observe ghetto life and to record it.

Epstein became a British citizen in 1912. In his autobiography, he referred to the sketches in this book: "I imagine that the feeling I have for expressing a human point of view, giving human rather than abstract implications to my work, comes from my early years on the East Side of New York."

# ten

# ODD CHARACTERS

No matter how unconventional are the numerous persons whom one can meet in the cafés of the quarter they are mainly redeemed by a genuinely intellectual vein. It is reserved for this final chapter to tell of some men who do not well fit into the preceding categories, but whose lives or works are, in one way or another, quite worthy of record.

---

Hapgood was more than generous in describing some of the characters he met on the Lower East Side. It was to be expected that a civilization given to so much talk would produce an odd-ball here and there and a little more odd than usual. Morris Rosenfeld, the poet, undertook to describe some of these oddballs in his essay, *The Nudnik*. A *nudnik* is not a translatable term. The word "bore" is accurate and the words "terrible bore" even more accurate. Perhaps no English word can do *nudnik* justice.

Says Rosenfeld of the *nudnik:*

"Most people are not always in a mood to argue; the *nudnik*, however, is forever on a search for ears to listen to his arguments, and the longer the ears the better he likes it.

"The *nudnik* is not limited to one type of *nudnik*-activity. The Creator has blessed him with all the psychic qualities needed for his chief virtue, his main purpose in life, his raison d'être—to bore the rest of humanity.

"He is a writer, a critic, a lecturer, a 'doer' and a reformer. He is a *nudnik* on all fronts and will bore you—and you—and anyone else who lets him.

"You sit and listen to him lecture and you must suck a lemon to keep from fainting; you lose your patience and would gladly beat him up for having the gall to charge a fee for wearying the public; the rickety chair on which you sit breaks under the weight of your burden, and you feel like doing violence to the newspaper which printed the announcement that brought you up to this godforsaken third-floor meeting room to hear a sermon on the 'Reasons for the Decadence of the String Bean.' You want to leap up on the platform, grab the *nudnik* by the legs, and hurl him back to Lithuania where he came from."

*N. M. Shaikevitch*

Shaikevitch is the author of interminable, unsigned novels which are published in daily installments in the East Side newspapers. He is so prolific that he makes a good living. There was a time, however, when he gladly signed his name to what he wrote. That time is over, and the reason for it is best brought out by a sketch of his history.

He was born in Minsk, Russia, of Orthodox Jewish parents. He began to write, when he was twenty years old, at first in pure Hebrew, scientific and historical articles. He also wrote a Hebrew novel called *The Victim of the Inquisition,* to which the Russian censor objected on the ground that it dealt with religious subjects.

Compelled to make his own living, young Shaikevitch, whose nom de plume has always been Schomer, began to write popular novels in Yiddish. At that time the Jews in Russia were, even more than now, shut up in their own communities, knew nothing of European culture, had an education, if any, exclusively Hebraic and medieval, and were outlandish to an extreme. The educated read only Hebrew, and the uneducated did not read at all. Up to that time, or until shortly before it, the Jew thought that nothing but holy teaching could be printed in Hebrew type. A man named Dick, however, a kind of forerunner of Shaikevitch, had begun to write secular stories in Yiddish. They were popular in form, intended for the ignorant populace who never read at all. Shaikevitch followed in Dick's lines, and made a great success.

He has written over one hundred and sixty stories, and for many years he was the great popular Yiddish writer in Russia. The people would read nothing but Schomer's works. The ignorant masses eagerly devoured the latest novel of Schomer's. It goes without saying that, under the circumstances, these books could be of very slight literary value. They were long, sentimental effusions, tales of bad Christians and good Jews, with a monotonous repetition of stock characters and situations, and with a melodramatic and sensational element. They probably corresponded pretty closely to our nickel novels, published in some of our cheapest periodicals, and intended for the most ignorant element of our population. Some of their titles are *A Shameful Error, An Unexpected Happiness, The Princess in the Wood, Convicted, Rebecca.*

Schomer was so successful that he had many imitators, who never, however, succeeded so well. The publishers sometimes tried to deceive the ignorant people into thinking that a new novel of Schomer's had appeared. On the cover of the book they put the title and the new author's name in very small letters, and then in very large letters, "In the style of Schomer." But it did not work. The people remained faithful to the books of the man whom they had first read.

When Shaikevitch, or Schomer himself, describes the purpose and characters of his work he talks as follows:

"My works are partly pictures of the life of the Jews in the Russian villages of fifty years ago, and partly novels about the old history of the Jews. Fifty years ago the Jews were more fanatical than they are now. They did nothing but study the Talmud, pray and fast, wear long beards and wigs, and look like monkeys. I satirized all this in my novels. I tried to teach the ignorant Jews that they were ridiculous, that they ought to take hold of modern, practical life and give up all that was merely formal and absurd in the old customs. I taught them that a pious man might be a hypocrite, and that it is better to do good than to pray. My works had a great effect in modernizing and educating the ignorant Jews. In my stories I pictured how the Jewish boy might go out from his little village into the wide, Gentile world, and make something of himself. In the last twenty-five years, the Jews, owing to my books, have lost a great deal of their fanaticism. At that time they had nothing but my books to read, and so my satire had a great effect."

Shaikevitch is not entirely alone in this good opinion of his work. Dr. Blaustein, superintendent of the Educational Alliance, said that he owed his position as an educated and modern man to reading novels when he was a boy. Dr. Blaustein lived in a small Russian village, and one day he read a story of Schomer's, which represented a Jewish boy going out into the world and critizing his Hebraic surroundings. That was the beginning of Dr. Blaustein's "awakening." Other intelligent Russian Jews probably had this same experience, although now as mature men they would all, no doubt, grant only a very small, if any, artistic quality to the famous Yiddish writer.

A few years after Shaikevitch's great popularity, two men began to write in Yiddish stories which really had value for the intelligent and educated—Abramovitch and, particularly, his pupil Rabinovitch. It was this work which, in some sort of form, did intelligently for the more educated Jews what Shaikevitch had done for the lowest stratum. Rabinovitch published a book in which he brought Shaikevitch to trial. He literally "tore him up the back" as far as literature is concerned—pointed out the tasteless, cheap, sensational character of his work, and held him up generally to ridicule.

As the Jews became better educated, this critical feeling about Shaikevitch's work grew more general. It is significant of the progress toward modern things made by the Jews that even the very ignorant no longer admire Shaikevitch's work as much as formerly. He is out of date, so much so that he now does not sign the stories he publishes in the Yiddish newspapers, which, nevertheless, are still popular among the most ignorant.

The intellectual socialists of the Jewish quarter in New York also had their fling at the popular writer, and helped to put him into obscurity. Now it is a common thing in the ghetto to hear a socialist say that Shaikevitch wielded a more disintegrating and unfavorable influence on the Jews than any other writer. But, nevertheless, the calm old man, who has a wife, and several grown children who are making their way in the new world, still sits quietly at his desk, drinking Russian tea and doing his daily "stunt" of several thousand words for the Yiddish newspapers.

The reason given by Mr. Shaikevitch for coming to America is that he began to be interested in playwriting, when the Yiddish stage was prohibited in Russia. The actors left Russia then and came to America, and some of them later wrote Shaikevitch, who was one of the earliest Yiddish playwrights, to join them in New York. He did so, and has written twelve plays, which have been produced in this city. Some of the better known of them are *The Jewish Count*, *Hamann the Second*, *Rebecca*, and *Dreyfus*. Shaikevitch is interesting mainly as representing in his work an early stage of the popular Yiddish consciousness.

## A CYNICAL INVENTOR

The intellectuals who gather in the Russian cafés delight in expressing the ideas for which they were persecuted abroad. Enthusiasm for progress and love of ideas is the characteristic tone of these gatherings and an entire lack of practical sense.

Very striking, therefore, was the attitude of a Russian-Jewish inventor, who took his lunch the other day at one of the most literary of these cafés. Near him were a trio of enthusiasts gesticulating over their tea, but he sat aloof, alone. He listened with a cold superior smile. He neither smoked nor drank, but sat, with his thin, shrewd face, chillily thinking.

It is common report in the community of the intellectual ghetto that Mr. Okun made a great invention connected with the electric arc lamp. It resulted in lengthening the time before the carbon is burned out from four or five hours to one hundred and fifty hours or thereabouts. He might have been a millionaire today, both he and his acquaintances maintain, but, with the usual unpractical nature of the Russian Jew, he was cheated by unscrupulous lawyers. He was a shirtmaker, and for six years saved from his ten dollars a week to buy the apparatus necessary for the task. At last it was completed, but he was robbed of the fortune, of the fame, of the prestige to which his great idea entitled him. As it is, he gets only twelve hundred and fifty dollars a year for the great deed, spends much of his time silently in the cafés, and dreams of other inventions when not engaged with criticizing his kind.

An American who sometimes visited the place for color and for the unpractical enthusiasm which he missed among his own people, sat down by the inventor, whose face interested him, and entered into conversation. He spoke of a Yiddish playwright whom he admired.

"I do not know much about him," said the inventor. "I am not a genius, like the others."

He sneered, but it was so nearly imperceptible that it did not seem ill-natured.

"But I am told," said the American, "that you are a great inventor. And that is a kind of genius."

"Yes, perhaps," he replied carelessly. "It takes talent, too, to do what I have done. But I am not a genius, like these people."

Again he smiled, sarcastically.

"I find," said the American, "a great many interesting people in these cafés."

"Yes, they are what you call characters, I suppose," he said dispassionately, "but I find them interesting only for one reason—no, no, I won't tell you what that reason is."

"You don't seem to be as enthusiastic about the people as I am," said the American, "but whenever I come into a café down here I find serious men who will talk seriously. They are different from the Americans who amuse themselves in bars, at horse races, and farces."

The inventor smiled coldly.

"I do not call serious what you call serious," he said. "It is not necessary to talk seriously to be serious. Serious men do things. The Russians don't do things. If they were gay and did things, they would be more serious than they are. But they are solemn and don't do anything."

"I don't agree with you," said the American warmly. "Doesn't Blank, who writes so many excellent novels, do anything? Don't the actors who act so truthfully, without self-consciousness, do anything? Don't the journalists who spread excellent ideas do anything?"

The inventor nodded judicially and remarked that there were some exceptions.

"But," he added, "you are deceived by the surface. There are many men in our colony who seem to be stronger intellectually than they really are. In Russia a few men, really cultivated and intellectual, give the tone, and everybody follows them. In America, however, the public gives the tone, and the playwright, the literary man, simply expresses the public. So that really intellectual Americans do not express as good ideas as less intellectual Russians. The Russians all imitate the best. The Americans imitate what the mass of the people want. But an intellectual American is more intellectual than these geniuses around here whom you like. Of course, they have some good things in them, as everybody has."

"What is it that you find to like in this Russian colony?" asked the American.

"I find," replied the inventor, "that when they come over here they lose what is best in the Russian character and acquire what is worst in the American character."

"And what do you deem best in the Russian character?"

"Well, in Russia they are warmhearted and friendly. They are envious even there, but not nearly so envious as they are here."

"And what do you find that is worst in the American character?"

"Oh, you know. They do everything for money. But yet there is more greatness in the American character. They are mechanical. They are practical. They don't get cheated by unscrupulous lawyers."

"Are you married?" asked the American sympathetically.

"No, thank God!" he replied, with more energy than he had yet shown.

"But you have no friends?"

"No."

"Some men," commented the American, "find a friend in a wife."

"That depends on a man's character. It increases the loneliness of some men," replied the inventor, smiling in spite of what he was saying.

"You seem to me to be rather pessimistic," remarked the American.

"No, I am not pessimistic. I understand that a pessimist thinks life is worse than it is, but I see things just as they are—that is all. When I came to New York, I was enthusiastic, too. I was an optimist. I saw life as it is not. But the mists have passed from before my eyes, and I see things just as they are."


AN IMPASSIONED CRITIC


He loves literature with an absorbing love, and is pained constantly by what he deems the chaos of art in the United States. The Americans seem to him to be trivial and immature in their art, lacking in serious purpose.

"It is a vast and fruitful land," he will say, "but

there is no order and little sincerity as far as art is concerned. Your writers try to amuse the readers, to entertain them merely, rather than to give them serious and vital truth. Why is it that a race which is clever and progressive in all mechanical and industrial matters, which in such things has no overpowering respect for the past, is weighed down in art by a regard for all the literary ghosts of bygone times? Look at the books put forth in any one year in the United States! What a senseless hodgepodge it is! Variety of all kinds, historical novels, short stories, social plays, costume plays, bindings, illustrations, *editions de luxe,* new editions of books written in all ages alongside of the latest productions of the day. The Americans have great tact in most things. They are the cleverest people in the world, and yet they are very backward in literature.

"Indeed the whole Anglo-Saxon race, great economically and practically as it is, is curiously at sea and chaotic in all that pertains to literary art. There are men of genius, great artists among them, but they are artists only in part, fragmentarily, artists without being aware of it, with no consistent and clear understanding of what art is. Your great men are hindered by their environment. America and England are the most difficult countries in the world for real art to get a hearing, for all the people insist on being amused by their authors. They treat them as they do their actors, merely as public servants whose duty it is to amuse the public when it is tired. But art is a serious thing, instinct with sincerity, and should never be lightly approached either by the artist or the reader.

"Another indication of what I mean is the way you all talk about style over here, as if the style had anything to do with art. Some of the great Russian realists have no style, but they are great artists. There was a time when to write well was an exception, and people who did it were supposed to be great. Now so many write well that it constitutes no longer any particular distinction. Real art consists in the presentation of ideas in images, and in the power of seeing in images, and of reproducing imaginatively. What is thus seen is wholly independent of style. And, more, words often stand in the way of art. A man writes a pretty style. There may be no idea or image beneath it, but you Anglo-Saxons say, 'Ha! Here is a man with a style, a great artist!' But he is no artist. He is a mere decorator, trivial and empty. He doesn't seize earnestly upon life and tell the truth about it. Now and then, indeed, I see indications of real art in your writers—great images, great characters, great truth —but all merely in suggestion. You don't know when you do anything good, and most of you don't like it when you see it. You prefer an exciting plot to a great delineation of character. Sometimes you throw off, often in newspapers, something that indicates great talent, real art, but you cover it up with an indistinguishable mass of rubbish. You don't know what you are after. You have no method. Every writer goes his single way, confused, at cross-purposes. There is no school of literature. Consequently, there is great loss of energy, great waste of material. There is great richness, but what carelessness, what deplorable carelessness, about the deepest and noblest and most serious things in life! I love you. I love you all. You are clever, good fellows, but you are children, talented, to be sure, but wayward and vagrant children, in the fields of art. Sincerity, realism, purpose, and unity are what as a race you need, if you wish ever to have a consistent and genuine art.

"The Russian, the Frenchman, the German, knows what he wants. He is after the truth. He is serious about life. He doesn't try to dodge the facts for the sake of a little false cheerfulness and optimistic inanity."

Thus talks the Russian prophet. He is a robust, earnest man, who is trying to make head and tail out of contemporary English literature. He finds no great mainspring of impulse or principle behind it, but an infinite pandering to an infinitely diversified public taste. He thinks it is a kind of vaudeville of art, full of compromises, vulgar in its lack of principle. It makes him sad in much the same way that skepticism and profanity sadden a deeply religious person. Wisdom and truth he wants, and doesn't find them. What he finds is haste, greed, incompleteness, and waste, and his soul abhors anything which takes away from the deepest nature of the soul. He is really a religious man, profound and sincere, sad at the wasteful, foolish lightness in art of the Anglo-Saxon world. Like his great countryman Tolstoy, he writes stories, and, again like Tolstoy, as he grows older the more he sees in art and life which he would like to reform and deepen. Economy of the heart, soul, and brain, the direction of them to a constant end—the feeling of the necessity of this is now an altruistic passion with this man. Like all reformers, he is sad, but, again like all reformers, he is robust and calm, self-sufficient.

## THE POET OF ZIONISM

Naptali Herz Imber is known to all Jews of any education as the man who has written in the old Hebrew

*Naptali Herz Imber*

language the poems that best express the hope of Zion and that best serve as an inspiring battle cry in the struggle for a new Jerusalem. Zangwill has translated into English the Hebrew *"Wacht Am Rhein,"* the most popular of Imber's poems, which is called *The Watch on the Jordan.* It is in four stanzas, the first of which is:

*Like the crash of the thunder*
*Which splitteth asunder*
*The flame of the cloud,*
*On our ears ever falling,*
*A voice is heard calling*
*From Zion aloud:*
*"Let your spirits' desires*
*For the land of your sires*
*Eternally burn*
*From the foe to deliver*
*Our own holy river,*
*To Jordan return."*
*Where the soft flowing stream*
*Murmurs low as in dream,*
*There set we our watch.*
*Our watchword, "The sword,*
*Of our land and our Lord,"*
*By the Jordan then set we our watch.*

Mr. Imber is a peculiar character and is said to be the original of the poet Pinchas in Zangwill's *The Children of the Ghetto.*

At a Russian-Jewish café on Canal Street he may often be found. Not long ago I met him there and discovered that the dignified Hebrew poet had as a man many of the more humorous and less impressive peculiarities of the character in Mr. Zangwill's book. It is difficult to take him seriously. He was sitting opposite an old *magid* (wandering preacher), whose specialty is to attack America, and he consented to tell about his work and to confide some of his ideas.

"I am the origin of the Zionistic movement," he said. "It is not generally known, but I am. Many years ago I went to Jerusalem, saw the misery of the people, felt the spirit of the place, and determined to bring my scattered people again together. For twelve years I struggled to put the Zionistic movement on foot, and now that I have started it I will let others carry it on and get the glory. For long I was not recognized, but when my Hebrew poems were published our whole race were made enthusiastic for Zion.

"If you wish to know what the spirit and purpose of my Hebrew poems is I will tell you. For two thousand years Hebrew poetry has been nothing but lamentations—nothing but literature expressing the spirit of Jeremiah. There have been no love songs, no wine songs, no songs of joy, nothing pagan. There have been no poets, only critics in rhyme. Now what I did in my Hebrew verses was to do away with lamentations. We have had enough of lamentations. I introduced the spirit of love and wine, the pagan spirit. My theme, indeed, is Zion. I am an individualist. It is the only *ist* I believe in, and I want my nation to be individual, too. I want them to be joyously themselves, and so I am a Zionist. Therefore I did away with critical poetry and with lamentations and led my people on to an individual and a joyous life."

Although Mr. Imber's best work is in Hebrew poetry, he is yet a very voluminous writer on science, economics, medicine, mysticism, history, and many other subjects.

"I have written on everything," said the poet. "Everything. I know almost nothing about the subjects on which I write. I don't believe in reading. I believe in knowing myself. In that way we learn to know others. Psychology is the only science. All others are fakes, and I can fake as well as anybody. Why read, or why seek amusement in the theaters or elsewhere, when one can sit in a café and talk to a man like that?"

He pointed at the old *magid* opposite him.

"Whenever I want to amuse myself," he said, "I talk to a man like that, and I cannot amuse myself without learning more about psychology."

With the exception of his poems, most of the poet's work was written in the English language.

"I began to write English late in life," he said. "Israel Zangwill helped me to begin. He said he would correct what I wrote, but I wrote so much that Mr. Zangwill stopped reading it and told me to go ahead on my own hook. So I did. I have written infinitely in English, some of which has been published: *Music of the Psalms; Education and the Talmud,* which was issued by the United States government in the report of the commissioner of education; many articles on mysticism and other subjects in the magazine *Ariel; The Mystery of the Golden Calf; The*

*Music of the Ghetto,* and many other works on cabalistic mysticism. I have also written *Who Was Crucified?* wherein I prove that it was not Jesus. If I kept on all day I could not tell you the names of all I have written. I have published many articles in the Jewish-American papers satirizing the rabbis, who consequently hate me. Much of my work, indeed, is satirical. The world needs cleaning up a little, particularly the rabbis. Put the Reformed and Orthodox rabbis together and some good might come of them. I am not afraid of these people, whom I call silk-chimney rabbis, because they wear tall hats instead of knowing the Talmud. It was my own invention—'silk-chimney rabbis.' "

Mr. Imber is evidently very fond of this phrase, for he repeated it many times. Indeed, he does not seem to be a very pious Jew. He himself admits it, for he said:

"I do not think they will say *Kaddish* for my soul when I am dead. And yet I am not a skeptic, exactly. I have a principle—Zionism. And beyond Zionism I have another great interest. I have now perfected Zionism, so I am free to pass on to mysticism, in which I am deeply at work. The mystics are all bluffers. I am a mystic, but my mysticism is simple and plain. My aim is to present a perfectly simple view of occultism. It is difficult to persuade Americans to become mystics. They care nothing for Hegel and Kant. Their philosophy I call Barnumism."

Mr. Imber has largely given up writing Hebrew now, but lately he wrote a Hebrew poem comprising two hundred closely printed pages. He did it, he said, to spite a man who said the poet had forgotten Hebrew because of his penchant for English.

Not long ago Mr. Imber wrote a "Last Confession" in Hebrew. He was very sick in a St. Louis hospital with blood poisoning, and thought he was going to die. They wanted him to confess his sins. So he did it, in Hebrew verse, which he translated to me, evidently on the spur of the moment, thus:

*When my day will come*
 *To wander in distress,*
*Call the priest to my room,*
 *My sins to confess.*

*The sins which I have committed*
 *With deliberation,*
*They will by the Lord be omitted,*
 *Who promised us salvation.*

*The evils I have done,*
 *Not conscious of the action,*
*Have passed away and gone*
 *Without satisfaction.*

*I see near me the green table:*
 *The gamblers play aloud,*
*And I am sick and unable*
 *To mix up with the crowd.*

*There are still beautiful roses,*
 *With aroma blessed;*

*There are still handsome maidens,*
   *Whose lips I have not pressed.*

*This has me affected,*
   *I am full of remorse,*
*That of late I have neglected*
   *The girl and the roses.*

Written on what the poet thought was his death-bed, this satirical poem is almost as heroic as *The Watch on the Jordan*.

Mr. Imber has also written many original poems in English, which, however, he fears will not live. Many of them are satirical poems about American life and politics. When in Denver before the Spanish war he wrote some verses beginning:

*Our flag will soon be planted*
*In a land where we do not want it.*

It was, the poet said, through the simple, clear character of his mystical attainments that he was able to predict the results of the war with Spain.

Mr. Imber looks upon America as the "land of the bluff" and as such admires it. But he disapproves of our reform movements. He thinks the recent attempt to reform the East Side was due to the desire of the rich to divert attention from their own vices. He doesn't approve of reform any way.

"We have been trying to reform human nature," he said, "for two thousand years, and have not done it yet. The only way to make a man good is to remove his stomach, for so long as he is hungry he will steal, and so long as he has other desires he will commit other wicked actions. Moses and Jesus were smart men and knew that evil could not be rooted out, and so they tolerated it."

Mr. Imber has recently made his last will and testament. It is in Hebrew prose and runs thus in English:

"To the rabbis I leave what I don't know; it will help them to a longer life. To my enemies I leave my rheumatism. Between the Republican and Democratic parties I divide the boodle which they have not yet touched. To the Jewish editors I leave my broken pen, so that they can write slowly and avoid mistakes. My books—those intended for beginners—I leave to the eight professors, so that they can learn to read. As an executor there shall be apppointed a man who knows Barnum's philosophy through and through. Written on my deathbed. Witness, Mr. Pluto of the Underground and his Famulus, the doctor. As an afterthought I leave to my publishers the last bill unpaid by me. They can frame it and keep it as an amulet to ward away that class of authors."

"Is it sarcastic?" asked Mr. Imber, chuckling delightedly.

Some time ago Mr. Imber sent the news of his own death to the various Hebrew and Yiddish publications. Many long obituaries—"very fine ones," said the poet—appeared.

"In that way," said Mr. Imber, "I learned who were my enemies. It had one evil consequence, however.

When I afterward asked the editor to publish one of my articles he said, 'You are officially dead, and as such cannot rush into print.'

"That reply really gave me a grievous moment," said the poet, with a shrewd Voltairean smile.

## AN INTELLECTUAL DEBAUCHEE

Four men sat excitedly talking in the little café on Grand Street where the socialists and anarchists of the Russian quarter were wont to meet late at night and stay until the small hours. An American, who might by chance have happened there, would have wondered what important event had occurred to rasp these men's voices, to cause them to gesticulate so wildly, to give their dark, intelligent faces so fateful, so ominous an expression. In reality, however, nothing out of the ordinary had happened. It was the usual course of human affairs which kept these men in a constant glow of unhappy emotion; an emotion which they deeply preferred to trivial optimism and the content founded on philistine well-being. They were always excited about life, for life as it is constituted seemed to them very unjust.

It was nearly midnight, and the men in the café, although they had drunk nothing stronger than Russian tea, talked on, seemingly intoxicated with ideas. One was the editor of a Yiddish newspaper in the quarter and a contributor to the anarchistic monthly. He was a man of about forty years of age, lighter in complexion than his companions, but yet dark. Like them he was dressed carelessly and poorly. In his melancholy eyes shone a gentle idealism. He spoke in a voice lower and softer than those of his fellows. He was deeply liked by them, for he was capable of sweet and beautiful ideas about the perfect humanity, some of which he had put into a play which had a short life on the Bowery but lived in the hearts of these warm intellectuals. Nonresistance to evil was the favorite principle of this gentle anarchist, whose name was Blanofsky.

His companions were younger and more heated and violent in speech, though their attenuated bodies and thoughtful and sensitive faces did not suggest reliance on physical force. On the Bowery the Irish tough fights after a word, but an all-day dispute between two Jews on Canal Street or Hester Street is unaccompanied by the clenching of a fist. A dark, thin young man, whose closely shaven face seemed somehow to fit his spirit, given over entirely to the movement, sat at Blanofsky's right hand. At almost any hour of the day or night Hermann Samarovitch could be found at the anarchist headquarters on Essex Street, poring over the books of the propaganda and engaging in talk with other bright spirits of the movement. Now, as he talked or listened in the café on Grand Street, his pale, smooth face seemed dead to all the ordinary interests of youth. The spirit of life was represented in him only by the passion for the cause, which burned in his black eyes. He had no other function than to worship at the shrine. How he lived, therefore, was a mystery.

Of the other two men, one, Jacob Hessler, a labor

leader in the ghetto, an eloquent speaker, of more commanding presence, but less sensitive and impressive at short range than either Blanofsky or Samarovitch, was silent, for the most part. He talked only to crowds, partly because it was exciting, but mainly because his limited intelligence put him at a disadvantage in intimate talk with men of concentrated intellectual character. The fourth man in the café, Abraham Gudinsky, was a simple admirer of Blanofsky. He was born in Jerusalem, had studied law in Constantinople, had lived in Paris as a bohemian, and, after a few years passed in the commonplace, dissipated gaiety of youth, had come to New York, where his sympathetic and idealistic character had come under the influence of the quiet charm of Blanofsky. He had small, alive eyes and a high forehead, and his body perpetually moved nervously.

"I do not believe," said Blanofsky in Russian, "that anything can be accomplished by force. Our cause is too sacred to tarnish it with blood, and it is too strong in logic and justice not to conquer peaceably in the end, and that, too, without leaving behind it the ill-breeding weeds of a violent course. I have nothing but pity for the misguided wretch who took the life of King Humbert, thinking he was acting for the cause. It is the acts of such madmen as he that make us appear to the public as merely irrational monsters."

"Nevertheless," said Samarovitch, his dark eyes glowing, "it is natural that the crimes of society against the individual should irritate us sometimes into violent acts. I am not sure but that it is good that it should be so. Those devoted men, in the great

*Sabina and Levitzky enter the café*

movement in Russia, at the time the czar was killed, were as clear-headed as they were devoted, and they felt that the governmental evil pressing in Russia could be relieved only by a kind of terrorism. And they were right," he concluded with gloomy emphasis.

Blanofsky shook his head, and was about to speak of Tolstoy, whom he regarded as the great interpreter of genuine anarchy, when he was interrupted by the approach of a young man and a young woman who had just entered the café. Sabina, as she was familiarly known to the faithful, dark and slender, with very large, emotional eyes and a mobile mouth, had just come from her lecture to a crowd of workingmen, to whom she had spoken eloquently of their right to lead a life with greater light and beauty in it.

The emotions expressed by her eloquence, and stirred by it, still lay in her deep eyes as she entered the café. Her companion, who had walked with her from the lecture, was a young poet, whose words followed one another with turbulent energy. His head was set uncommonly close to his compact, stout shoulders, seeming to have a firmer rest than usual on the trunk, and thus better to support the strain of his thick-coming fancies. His habitual attitude was to hold his closed fist even with his shoulder, and punctuate with it the transitions of his thought. Even in winter the perspiration rolled down his face as he spoke, for thought with him was intense to the point of pain. He was the perfect type of the intellectual debauchee of the Russian-Jewish colony. He drank nothing but tea and coffee, but within him burned his ideas. He made his living by writing an occasional poem or article for a Yiddish paper, and when he had gathered together a few dollars he repaired again to the cafés, seeking companions to whom he could confide his exuberant thoughts, which were always expressed in poetic images. He slept whenever and wherever he was tired, but he slept seldom and unwillingly. Unrest was his quiet and unhappiness his dearest consolation. The type of his mind was as Russian as his name, which was Levitzky. The girl looked and listened to him, fascinated. They sat down at the table with the others, and while the waiter was bringing their tea and lemon, Levitzky continued his discourse:

"No, I do not like America. The people here are satisfied. Things seem frozen here—finished. Great deeds have been done, great things have been created. Wall Street and Broadway fill me with wonder. The outside is great, showing energy that has been. But at the core, all is dead. The imagination and the heart are extinguished. Content and comfort eat up the nation. New York seems to me an active city of the dead, where there is much movement, but no soul. Russia, which I love, is just the opposite. There nothing is done, nothing finished. One sees nothing, but feels warmth and vitality at the heart. In love it is the same way. The American wants a legal wife and a comfortable home, but the Russian wants a mistress behind a mountain to whom he cannot penetrate but toward whom he can strive, for whom he can long and dream. It is better to hope than to attain."

Sabina looked at him, her bosom heaving. His last words seemed to trouble her, but she sat in silence and appeared to listen to the conversation, which turned on a recent strike in the ghetto. Finally she got up to go home, refusing Levitzky's offer to accompany her. Leaving the anarchists still engaged in talk, she went into the street, which, although it was after one o'clock, was still far from deserted.

Instead of going to her poor room in the tenement house on Hester Street Sabina walked slowly along Grand Street toward the Bowery, deep in reflection. She was thinking of Levitzky and of her life. Ten years before, as a child of twelve, she had come to New York from Russia with her father, a tailor, who had worked for several years in the sweatshops. He had died two years before, and since then Sabina had worked in the sweatshops in the day time and in the evening had devoted herself to the cause. At first she had gone to the socialistic and anarchistic meetings merely because they were attended by the only society in the East Side which at all satisfied her growing intellectual activity. These rough working-men sometimes seemed to her inspired, and her ardor and youth were soon deeply interested in the cause of socialism, partly because of the pity inspired by the sordid poverty about her, but mainly because of the strong attraction any earnest movement has for a young and emotionally intellectual person. As was quite inevitable, she went from an unreserved love for the group of ideas called socialistic to the quite contrary ones of anarchy. And this change was not founded on intellectual conviction, but was due to the simple fact that the anarchistic cause was more extreme and gave greater apparent opportunity for self-sacrifice, and for the reason, too, that the most interesting man she had met, Levitzky, was at that time an anarchist. These two made, very often, passionate speeches on the same evening to a crowd of attentive laborers, and after the meeting walked the street together or sat over their tea in the café discussing high ideals, not only anarchy, but all noble subjects that detach the soul from the sordid business of life.

Of course, Sabina loved Levitzky. His robust intellect and exuberant, poetical nature, a nature constant to passion, but inconstant to persons, made her beloved ideas seem real, gave a concrete seal to the creations of her imagination.

Neither Levitzky nor Sabina was conscious of the strong feeling that he was arousing in the girl's soul. He poured his mind out to her. His rich nature unfolded in her sympathetic presence. She loved him for the mental crises he had passed; and he loved merely the mental images his words aroused in him when she was present.

It was not until the evening of the scene in the café that she had fully understood that she was eternally in love with Levitzky. On the walk from the lecture to the Grand Street café they had for the first time spoken of love between man and woman, and Levitzky had launched forth into an eloquent tirade against satisfied desire, a speech which was concluded in the café, with the remark about how a Russian loves an inaccessible mistress, a beautiful creature separated from her lover by a mountain, while the despised American wants a legal wife whom he can enjoy and be sure of.

The sentiment fitted in beautifully with Sabina's habitually enthusiastic habit of mind. But tonight she was ashamed of herself because his words filled her with fear and pain. Irrational emotion drove her theories from her head, and struck her dumb with grief for what she looked upon as a betrayed ideal. She, who had devoted herself to the movement; she, who had chosen an intellectual career, a life devoted to the cause of humanity; she, who had been proud of her independence and had confidently looked forward to a life of celibacy—this superior person was in love, and loved as passionately and as personally as any commonplace woman. She devoutly believed in the worth of Levitzky's ideas against human love between the sexes, and the fact that her nerves and imagination went against her head overwhelmed her with remorse. She was unfaithful not only to her own ideals, but to the ideals of the man she loved. She knew that Levitzky felt no love for her. If he had, she would not have loved him. She longed to tear this feeling, which she felt to be unworthy of her and in the nature of an insult to him, from her heart. But she knew she could not.

After leaving Levitzky and the anarchists in the café, Sabina walked slowly toward the Bowery, suffering with love and humiliation, thinking of Levitzky and of the past, the devoted past which now seemed deeply wronged. Her despair can perhaps be understood by the fanatical nun whose years of devotion to her vows are rendered vain by a sudden impulse of the heart which is yielded to, or by the ambitious man of affairs who betrays a governmental trust because of the repeated frenzy of an emotion which wears out his resistance and leads him to the woman who has charmed and deceived him.

As Sabina passed through the street her attention was mechanically caught by the notice in a shop window, which was still dimly lighted, of an important labor meeting, to take place in a couple of days, at which a famous German anarchist was to speak —a man who was coming from Europe to join the movement in New York, whose books she had read and loved. Such notices always arrested her eager attention, and even now habit led her to stop by the window and dully read the entire poster. The thought of the coming event, which would once have been of palpitating interest to her, increased her remorse and despair. Of such great activity as this she had rendered herself incapable. To go to any such meeting now would be hypocrisy, she felt. The cause she wanted to love and serve and still did love she could yet never again be wholehearted about. She bore with her a burden. She seemed to herself to be a sinful creature, and the devoted life she had led seemed poisoned by this terrible passion which controlled her. She felt she never again could look Levitzky in the face, for a terrible impulse in her was about to drag her from the pedestal where he had helped to place her, and to drag with her the man she loved from the impersonal height at which he stood.

Her passionate nature rebelled at the thought of any compromise with the ideal. She could not endure life otherwise than as her imagination dictated—and here was a passion which threatened the existence of all she approved. What in a colder nature would have been a mere intellectual phase was with her an unbearably emotional upheaval; and on the spot she made a resolution conceived in despair but carried out with logical coolness. As the rebellious thought surged over her and filled her being with hot emotion, she became aware that the shop was that of an apothecary on East Broadway, whither she had unconsciously wandered. With set lips she entered, aroused the sleeping clerk, a socialist whom she knew, and bought that which soon allayed her problem without solving it. Early the next morning the clerk found her lying near the doorway, with an expression of impulsive energy on her dark face.

About three days later Blanofsky and his three friends were sitting in the café on Grand Street, drinking their eternal Russian tea and talking about Levitzky.

"I never saw a man so broken," said Blanofsky in his soft voice, "as Levitzky was by the death of that girl. For a week I feared for his life, he was so desperate. It seems he met Lefeitkin's clerk, who told him. He disappeared from the quarter for several days, and no one knew where he went. Four days ago he came to my room looking like a madman. His hair was full of mud and his clothes torn and filthy. His eyes burned in his pale face, and his speech, more voluminous than ever, was broken and incoherent. He stayed all day, refused to eat, but talked all the time of Sabina, of her mind, of her rare personality, of her devotion to the cause. He was interrupted by fits of sobbing. I did not know that this man of intellect was capable of so great personal feeling."

"Levitzky is weak," said Herman Samarovitch, "and inconstant. He has vivid ideas, and imagination, but he never really cared for the cause. He was a socialist before he was an anarchist. Before that he was an atheist, which followed a period of religious mysticism. At one time he was a conventional capitalist in principle, with the English government as his model. He is easily moved by an idea or an emotion, but he easily passes to another. He will soon forget this girl's death, to which he should have been superior. He has no steadfastness, and is not one of us."

At this point, Levitzky entered the café. With him was the new arrival, the German anarchist. To him Levitzky was talking with great animation. His words rolled over one another with enthusiasm.

"Do you know," he said eagerly, his face beaming, to Blanofsky and his companions, "that our distinguished friend here has consented to debate tomorrow night with our socialist friend, Jacob Matz, that mistaken but able man, on the nature of individual right as interpreted by the anarchist on one side and the socialist on the other. I have written a poem on liberty which I intend to read at the meeting. Do you wish to hear it?"

He drew a manuscript from his pocket and read enthusiastically a poem in which a turbulent love for man and nature, for social equality and foaming cataracts was expressed in rich imagery. His face glowed and he seemed transported. He had forgotten Sabina.

free, 43
private. *See* chaider
Hebrew Technical Institute, 29, 30, 44
Hebrew Trades, United, 38
Heine, Moses, 154
Henry Street Settlement, 45, 175
*Herald*, 189, 190, 191
Hermalin, D., 197
Hessler, Jacob, 284
Hester Street, 53, 243, 247-249, 251, 253, 254, 258, 259, 284, 288
High Holy Days, xii, 10
Hillquit, Morris, 40
Hirsch
    Baron de, 30
    Baroness de, 30
home factories, garment manufacture in, 11-12
    *See also* sweatshops
Hopkins, Harry, 45
Horowitz, Professor M., 125, 127, 128, 130, 131, 134, 135, 153, 154, 168
Hospital, National Jewish, 95
housing developments, vi
Houston Street, 241
humor, ghetto, xiii, xiv, 6

Imber, Naptali Herz, 275-283
immigrants
    Irish, viii, ix
    Italian, viii, ix
    Jewish, vii, viii, xii
    Polish, ix, x
*Imported Bridegroom, The,* 233-234
intellectuals, 47-52, 79, 97, 114, 196, 261, 270, 283-294
International Ladies' Garment Workers' Union, 39
inventor, a cynical, 267-275

Janowsky, S., 192
Jerome, William Travers, 41
*Jewish King Lear,* 129, 169, 173
Jewish Desertion Bureau, xiii
*Jewish Morning Journal,* 185-186
Jewish Social Work, Training School for, 187
*Jewish World,* 189
Jolson, Al, 174

Kwartin (cantor), 75
Kalisch, Bertha, 132, 134, 168, 171, 172
Kalisch, Samuel, 256-257
Karb, Mrs., 153
Katz, ———, literary editor of *Vorwärts,* 194
Kessler, David, 133, 143, 154, 162, 165, 167, 171, 172
Kobrin, Leon, 217-222
*kosher* food, 72
    *See also* dietary laws
Kozelski (actor), 158
Kozlowski (actor), 158
Kranz, Philip, 197
Krilow (writer), 56
Kupfer, Israel, 151, 152

labor, singer of, 108-112
Labor Temple, 242
*Landsmanschaften,* 14
Lang, Harry, 188
Latteiner, Joseph, 125, 128, 130, 131, 140, 153, 154-156, 168, 170
Law, the, 21, 22, 25, 73, 74, 78, 92
    *See also* Talmud
Lazarus, Emma, 44
Lehman, Herbert H., 45
Lessin. *See* Wald, Abraham
Levin, ———, 207-211, 212, 217, 222
Levitzky, ———, 287-294
library, 32
Libin, S., 201-208, 211, 212, 215, 217, 218, 221, 222
Liptzen, Mrs., 165-168, 170, 171
literature, ghetto, place of women in, 90-92
lodges, 13
London, Meyer, 40
Look, The, 27
Loewenberg, Nathaniel, 257-258
Lower East Side of New York, vi, viii, xi, xii, xiii, 26
    changes in, xi
    immigration of Eastern European Jews to, vii
    small business success on, 13

Madison, House, 45
"Mail Wagon, The," 102
marriage, 94, 95